The Teaching
of Reading
-without
Really any
Method

The Danish Research Council for the Humanities has supported the publication of this manuscript. The authors have forgone their fees, which has made it possible to publish this book. Incidentally Piet Hein should be given thanks for his permission to illustrate this book with Grooks one of which was re-created in English especially for this book.

Mogens Jansen
Bo Jacobsen
Poul Erik Jensen

The Teaching of Reading -without Really any Method

An Analysis of
Reading Instruction in Denmark

Published by

MUNKSGAARD, COPENHAGEN
HUMANITIES PRESS INC., NEW JERSEY

The Teaching of Reading – without Really any Method,
1st edition, 1st printing
© 1978 by Mogens Jansen, Bo Jacobsen, Poul Erik Jensen
and Munksgaard, Copenhagen, Denmark
Cover and design by Ib K. Olsen
Drawings by Pjotr Baro
Foreword by Gaston E. Blom
Printed in Denmark by
ISBN-87-16-01617-3

Published simultaneously in the U.S.A.
by Humanities Press Inc.
ISBN-0-391-00878-1

Scandinavian University Books
Denmark MUNKSGAARD Copenhagen
Norway   UNIVERSITETSFORLAGET Oslo, Bergen, Tromsö
Sweden   ESSELTE STUDIUM Stockholm, Gothenburg, Lund

Authors

Mogens Jansen, b. 1930, cand. psych.
Mogens Jansen is the Director of the Department of Educational Experiments at The Danish Institute for Educational Research and leader of several projects under the Danish Research Council for the Humanities. He has been President of the Danish National Association of Reading Teachers since 1963. He has worked on many official committees and boards. In 1974 he was awarded The Special Service Award by the International Reading Association for his work to further the teaching of reading. Mogens Jansen was a classroom teacher in the primary and secondary schools at grade levels one through ten. He has had special education training. He has been an instructor at the Teachers' Training College, Royal Danish School of Educational Studies and Royal School of Librarianship. Mogens Jansen has published educational studies in Denmark and other countries and many books and articles on reading and language. He has developed many educational materials which are currently being used in the Danish primary and secondary schools. He is well known in the international reading field.

In this book Mogens Jansen is mainly responsible for chapters 1, 2, and 3.

Bo Jacobsen, b. 1940, *Ph. D.*
Bo Jacobsen is a psychologist who is also a reading specialist with considerable experience in teaching retarded and advanced students. For some years he has taught reading skills on the adult level. In the past Bo Jacobsen

5

was a classroom teacher in primary and secondary schools. He has been the leader of the reading and studying technical laboratory at The Royal School of Librarianship where he was Assistant Professor. He has worked as an educational consultant and group psychologist to the Royal Danish Academy of Arts and has made publications in the field of human development. He is now Assistant Professor at the Institute for Studies in Higher Education at the University of Copenhagen.

In this book Bo Jacobsen is mainly responsible for chapters 6, 7, and 8.

Poul Erik Jensen, b. 1940, *Ph. D.*
Poul Erik Jensen is Associate Professor at The Danish Institute for Educational Research where he is also the leader of a research group working on classroom analysis in social studies. He has taught at the Teachers' Training College and Royal Danish School of Educational Studies as well as within other sorts of education for a number of years. In the past he was a primary and secondary school teacher and a school psychologist. Poul Erik Jensen has been interested in the relationship of psychology and teaching particularly as this concerns reading instruction.

In this book Poul Erik Jensen is mainly responsible for chapters 4 and 5.

Foreword

It is a pleasure to write a foreword to this unusual and interesting book. The title "The Teaching of Reading– without Really Any Method", contains an element of humor, somewhat Danish in character. But the content of the book is not humorous, although a Danish style of writing and thinking pervades it. It indeed deals with an important topic and reports the Danish point of view and experience in reading. This is done modestly, thoughtfully and in a quiet, provocative way. The book is not replete with statistical findings and research studies, but those reported are particularly poignant.

I have had the good fortune to supervise the English translation of the original Danish text. The authors did the yeoman work of the first translation and I have attempted to modify it for English reading audiences. In so doing I have tried to preserve some of the essential flavors of the authors and to be true to their Danish way of expressing things. If I have not been entirely successful in this effort I apologize to the authors. My capacities in the Danish language are limited to a childhood Scandinavian ("børne-skandinavisk"). However, I have had the good fortune of meeting and working with the three authors of this book, especially during a recent sabbatical year in Denmark. So I have had some direct knowledge and experience with the topic of the book.

The professional background and experience of the three authors as summarized p. 5–6, condense their many qualifications to write such a book. All of them have been classroom teachers. They have done original research, singly and together, some of which has now become available in an international language (English). The authors maintain an active, practical and clinical, professional life in reading. Mogens Jansen in particular is active and well known in the international reading field. Bo Jacobsen and Poul Erik Jensen are both well known in Scandinavian reading circles.

The field of reading research is very much dominated by American and British research studies and publications. For this reason alone Danish studies and experience of many years in teaching reading should be made more visible. Perhaps this visibility may also correct an impression that reading is primarily an Anglo-American activity. Literacy, likewise, is not limited to the English language. Therefore it is important to make known that practiced literacy in Denmark is remarkably well developed. The authors indicate this may be partly the result of a national program in reading that began in 1958. However, this program was built upon already established principles of a holistic psychology and of a deep commitment to individual differences in children and adults.

"The Teaching of Reading—without Really Any Method" is written in a form that is loyal to the principle of reading for different purposes, one of the many central ideas advanced by the authors. This book has accomplished that characteristic very well indeed! Its structure and format make it possible to skim, scan, speed, obtain general impressions, and focus on topics of special interest. And if you like to rebus read, there are some charts, diagrams and tables. There is a content summary as well, which provides a condensed version of what the book contains. Each chapter has paragraph titles. However, the reader would be remiss if he or she overlooked the substantive content since there is much of universal interest to teachers and others concerned with the teaching of reading in various parts of the world. To paraphrase

8

Shakespeare, "There is something exciting in the State of Denmark."

In various parts of the book there are important concepts – ones which become even more profound when you think more deeply about them. It is not possible to cite them all, rather to illustrate a few that are in store for the reader. Regarding reading tests the authors indicate that "the demands of their reliability must be released in order to place more importance on the validity" of functional measures of reading ability. In discussing the arguments and debates on instructional methods in reading the authors refer to "method imperialism". In the concluding chapter an ethical issue is raised concerning the training of skilled effective adaptive readers. Might this have an influence on the personality such as developing a specific cognitive style? Might this not preserve individual differences in habits, attitudes and problem solving of human beings? The authors hope that methods of education can be formed which develop strong durable cognitive functioning but also foster varied and adaptable individual differences. "The either-or way of thinking may be thinking" but "maybe we should now and then think the as-well-as way". In the last sentence of the main text the fundamental basic attitude of this book is stated: "reading is important; in school it is extremely important but it is not *that* important." I can add nothing further of importance.

Gaston E. Blom.

M. D., Professor of Psychiatry, Michigan State University, Michigan, USA.

Contents

11

14

17

LITTLE CAT

Little cat,
little cat
walking all alone,
whose little cat
are you?
- I'm jolly well my own.

Introduction

Why read this book on reading instruction in Denmark?

"Why read this book on reading instruction in Denmark?"

"Well ..."

Question Number 1

"Because Denmark may be looked upon as a social laboratory where East and West meet? Because the United States and the Soviet Union will recognize some of their own characteristics and perhaps wonder how things can still be different?"

"No ... Not exactly for those reasons."

Question Number 2

"Does this concern education at all?"

"Yes."

"Because Denmark is a homogeneous society in a tangled world?"

Question Number 3
"Because Denmark is one of the few countries of the world having had only one language for centuries?

Where in general only one culture exists?

Where the pattern of life is not broken by significant subcultures?"

"No . . . Not exactly for those reasons."

Question Number 4
"Does it concern reading instruction?"

"Yes."

"Because Danmark traditionally has had an interest in the individual?

Because holistic psychology has been generally accepted and has influenced educational practice for years?"

"No . . . Not particularly for those reasons."

"Does the interest in individualization and holistic psychology concern reading instruction?"

"Yes."

Question Number 5
"Because Denmark has developed reading materials to an astonishingly extensive degree considering the small language area that is represented? Because people do not take exclusive interest in reading within reading instruction, i. e. reading is important, but not too important? Because educators concern themselves with language as a whole, the child as a whole, the pupil as a whole, and the situation as a whole?"

"Yes."

In Denmark Problems Can Be Viewed through a . . .
Reading instruction concerns the world of the child within his or her surrounding society. It concerns language, cultural heritage and communication and also the educational and psychological traditions.

20

Reading instruction in Denmark is a well-described phenomenon with all its good and bad qualities, its shortcomings and defects and its advantages. Other language areas and countries may see their own characteristics through a Danish magnifying glass.

... Magnifying Glass

The methods in mother tongue language instruction in general and in reading in particular can be evaluated, even though it might appear that one had not found the philosopher's stone: 'The right method'!

The Methods

And if the 'right method' – the philosopher's stone – was found, it might be necessary to discard the stone, because it appeared that – though glittering – it was not made of gold.

In this book there is not *one* method but several methods. There is no philosopher's stone but some general characteristics. The best method will never be found.

The development of materials in Denmark is associated with the fact that the language area is small. This is one of the circumstances enforcing realism. The Danes have maintained their educational goals, but at the same time they have been forced to consider economic realities. The result has been that materials are used very differently and very flexibly in education. Also the teacher has to emphasize other aspects of instruction than materials. One will never get 'the best material'.

The Materials

Reading is often used as one word as if it was only one very well-defined concept. When one looks upon reading as containing different 'forms of reading', it is possible to provide instruction which is appropriate for each stage. At the elementary stage reading is not reading but, as a rule, rebus-reading – cf. chapter 2.

Elementary Reading Instruction

As an extension of this point of view, remedial reading instruction can be seen more clearly. It is impossible to

Remedial Instruction

21

refer to "retarded" without at the same time referring to "retarded in relation to what?" It is necessary to specify what exactly is meant when saying "retarded". You must be able to describe what is normal and what is retarded before you start to treat – cf. chapter 3.

Individualiza-
tion

The problem of individualization exists in all countries. In Denmark it has been dealt with in another way than those generally used. Perhaps the point of departure is different? Or rather one aims at other solutions? – cf. chapter 4.

Advanced
Reading Skills
Training

Advanced reading training for young people and adults is probably the area in which a distinctive Danish character is most notable. Perhaps this is the result of a different psychological tradition – cf. chapter 5. Most likely this is also due to the influence of holistic educational approaches and an openness in the schools – cf. chapters 6 and 7. One cannot forget the students when one is discussing schools and education – and especially reading! What do students tell about their own reading? – cf. chapter 8.

So far reading instruction in Denmark has mainly gone its own way. Maybe it has gone astray? Maybe it has gone ahead? At any rate these introductory statements fit the reading instruction situation in Denmark:

LITTLE CAT

Little cat,
little cat
walking all alone,
whose little cat
are you?
-I'm jolly well my own.

He on whom
God's light does fall
sees the great things
in the small.

1.

A holistic educational approach to reading

No methodology or educational approach can be said to be "right" or "wrong" in itself. A methodology is a solution to a series of educational problems. It is based on particular conditions and on an educational philosophy. The educational approach described in this book arose from certain background conditions, uniquely characteristic for a small country like Denmark. But it is just as essential to question basic educational attitudes concerning how one looks at language and how one looks at the pupil, whether he or she is a child or an adult. Some of these conditions for 'open' and holistic educational practices are described in this chapter.

It is fundamental that learning to read is not looked upon as isolated in the education of a child. Reading in the mother tongue is considered a part of the child's general

Reading is Part of the Language

23

linguistic growth and development. This has proved a productive way of presenting the issues in reading. It fits the learning of other languages. The education in foreign languages is provided all Danish pupils later in their education (cf. p. 44).

Language Viewed in Four Stages

It is usual to describe general linguistic development as four successive links: listen → speak → read → write. But, necessarily, this sequence must also include 'understanding':

Listen + understand → listen + understand + speak → listen + understand + speak + read → listen + understand + speak + read and write *the language*.

This emphasizes that speaking or reading are not just mechanical factors, but parts of a general cognitive development.

Understanding and Listening

The transition between successive parts may be amplified. Listening to and understanding a language is the basis for all language learning. It is also the point of origin for the entire mother tongue instruction in school. During the last 20 years instruction has been inspired age-wise from below (kindergarten and kindergarten class), rather than from above (university and high school). This has resulted in an emphasis on understanding – listening – looking – hearing – speaking. This has had the effect that *part*-situations are not appreciated in daily work. Broad, total and meaningful learning experiences are preferred. These broad situations are difficult to formalize. The broad aim of daily work, consequently, leads to a relatively informal way of instruction.

Listening → Speaking

The next linkage, listening → speaking, is essential in many ways. Latent in learning to listen is a tolerance towards others. This behavior is socially valuable and has been developed by the open attitude, characterizing instruction in kindergarten and the first two or three years of school. Listening is not a single simple activity. It is

24

an ability which is practiced throughout the daily work in many different situations. It is a goal to strive for and forms a part of the ideals of the child. Speaking is not just exercises and absolutely not phonetic training. It is 'talk with' rather than 'speak to'. So the listening function is strongly represented as an absolute condition for learning to speak. You may easily speak to without listening, but you cannot talk with without listening. It sounds simple, but is essential.

Speaking → reading are also naturally attached. During the last few months' work in the kindergarten class an almost unnoticeable transition into the reading instruction of the 6- to 7-year-old children takes place.

Speaking →
Reading

Learning to read is mentioned frequently in this book – much more frequently than reasonable, considering the significance of this topic within the entire language. Other aspects of the acquisition of a language would be more significant within the entire educational picture. However, reading is the central topic of this book. Therefore there is a disproportionately large number of words on reading compared to the fewer words on listening, speaking, writing and understanding.

Reading and writing the language is the fourth linkage. The emphasis now changes slightly from reading to reading and writing. Gradually it becomes quite important to be able to write the language. This is not only a question of expressing some thoughts in written form, but also of the orthography. Probably the more mechanical aspects of writing itself should be more emphasized. However, for a couple of generations writing instruction has been a big empty hole in Denmark.

Reading →
Writing

There are always pupils, who 'get the worst of it'. It can be taken for granted that the more suitable material is available the better the teacher will be able to instruct each single pupil – at his or her actual level. And the

Last Numbers
in a Row
Always Exist

greater the investment in time and facilities the smaller the number of linguistically retarded pupils will be.

But it is essential to hold on to the fact that no matter how expediently one works with the entire learning of language, and especially with learning to read and learning to write within elementary school, one will never reach the dream-situation that there are no pupils with linguistic difficulties. There will still be pupils who'get the worsst of it'. This is seen clearly at the stage, where importance is placed on reading. It is just as clear at the stage of reading and writing the language.

They are Associated With Good Teaching

The continuous development towards the ideal of a better elementary school, especially more effective reading instruction and better mother tongue instruction in general, will lead to still greater educational demands. More will be expected from the linguistically weakest pupils in school as well. As better help is provided by the school, fewer problems should be expected at first. In a situation where the ordinary school renders the best possible education and where good progress is noted with most pupils according to their potentialities, the number of retarded readers will be smaller. School itself would not produce weak pupils by inadequate instruction or by instruction directed at certain pupils only. When ordinary education becomes "too good" (and that is only an idealistic possibility), a new problem in fact occurs. It is rather clearly reflected within mother tongue instruction in Denmark.

When new areas of education are started and new objectives are established (as for instance systematic reading and study skills training), there are good possibilities for helping the ordinary group of pupils further – from about 11–12 years of age and older. But the linguistically weakest are confronted with a new challenge. In this way one is placed in the bizarre situation that the better the education rendered to ordinary pupils is, the greater the need for special education of a weak group becomes. The more hurdles the pupils have to cope with the greater is the risk of stumbling.

Reading instruction may be a concrete example that the problem in individualization is not solved, even by granting the individual rather large possibilities. Special education and retarded children are attached to the demands made on how good ordinary education is or becomes.

In Denmark it is usual for educational debate to be stimulated by developments from other countries. But there is a long delay. Nowadays the discussion reaches us from abroad after about five years. Some years ago Anglo-American education began to talk about "subcultures" and this of course influenced Danish education. There was much discussion about and interest in "subcultures". The concept evoked a response among some of the teachers working with the children. But the discussion did not have realistic significance. The reason was that "subcultures" within the Danish language area are extremely limited compared with those of other countries. In Denmark there is really only one language within the borders of the country. The dialects function on the same level as folk dances in an open-air museum. Nobody wants to eliminate them. They are kept just barely alive. After all, you cannot administer artificial respiration to traditions. *One Language and One Culture*

The significance of dialects is now being discussed abroad. We shall have the same debate in Denmark in the late seventies – even though the basis of the discussion in Denmark is so fundamentally different from that of the foreign countries inspiring the debate that it will have no decisive factual meaning at all.

Denmark is also homogeneous as to race. Different groups such as gypsies in transit and small (but frequently discussed) groups of guest workers from Yugoslavia, Tur- *One Race*

27

key and Pakistan are usually not absorbed among the Danes. Many of them do not wish to be. The more or less voluntary guests, refugees from Eastern Europe, Asia and elsewhere, are so few in number that they do not play a significant role.

One 'subculture' differs remarkably: the Greenlanders who live in Greenland and those who have moved to other parts of Denmark. This amounts to a little more than 40,000 people.

Subcultures of a Different Type

In the 1930's the 'working-class culture' was discussed by intellectual groups. People with a sense of tradition were concerned with a 'farmer's culture', which they named "peasant culture".

But these subcultures have not been significant and were short lived. During the last decade one subculture after the other has emerged, characteristically with increasing speed (Toffler, 1970). The 'youth rebellion' has developed its culture, which has had a certain penetration. The intellectually borne 'student marxism' is firmly rooted in university institutions. The 'women's rebellion' is establishing its subculture, which at any rate until now has had more effect on the intellectual mass media than on the daily life of the nation. Several other examples of movements might be mentioned, for instance 'power for children', 'old-age pensioners' rebellion' and the so-called 'middle-aged people's rebellion'.

The fact is that whenever groups are so small, as they have to be in Denmark, the level at which quite a small number of persons have their own subculture is rather easily reached. Then we approach the point where people are divided as individuals instead of in subcultures. Thus educational practice is usually not durably influenced by the ideologies of subcultures. However, the demand for the individuality of each single person is not a trifling point to start from an instructional point of view.

28

A holistic psychology maintains that a whole is always more than the sum of its parts. The child's situation is not only the sum of its surroundings. A book is more than the sum of its words and paper. To psychologically well-informed teachers it sounds extremely old-fashioned to emphasize this. It is a truism. And it is a fact which psychologists have been aware of for many years. *A Danish Holistic Psychology*

What has characterized Danish psychology, as far as these issues are concerned, is a specific fear of injuring the everyday life of a school by splitting it into pieces to be studied and dealt with separately. On the contrary, what has been attempted is to describe and to work concretely with units, which are perceived as meaningful wholes. This has become a general approach in Danish psychology and has had a perceptible effect on Danish educational tradition. The Danish school psychologists have also dealt with the entire child, not primarily with dysfunctions (Tarnopol, 1976).

This comprehensive view of the child corresponds to the educational philosophy that it is the task of the teacher to create optimal conditions for the child to develop by himself or herself. The task is not to shape the child for specific purposes. In this respect the teacher might be better compared to a gardener, creating good conditions of growth for his plants, than to a sculptor modeling his clay. Some reject this view of the child with inherent possibilities. They reject it as weak-willed and non-goal-directed. Still, it is a basic attitude which has marked Danish education and Danish methodology in mother tongue education as described in this book. *Faith in the Child's Possibilities*

Other features which characterize Danish educational thought will be discussed in subsequent chapters. These include the belief in 'learning-by-doing' and the rejection of belief in 'the right methods' or 'the right materials'.

Knowing what
thou knowest not
is in a sense
omniscience.

2.

Reading instruction at school

There Are
Many Kinds
of Reading

Instruction in reading is a natural part of entire linguistic training, described in the previous chapter. Systematic reading instruction in a more traditional sense usually starts during the first year of school; as a rule during the first half year. Reading instruction continues in principle throughout the entire schooling of the pupil.

About twenty years ago reading instruction existed only during the first two years of school. After that there was oral reading training for one or two years. From the fourth year of school reading instruction was more or less casual as far as reading technique is concerned. The basic element was not reading but passing on cultural heritage and, often too early, attempting to introduce adult literature.

Rebus-Reading

There are many kinds of reading. One form is rebus-reading. The concept 'rebus-reading' was introduced in

30

Denmark in 1959 (Jansen, 1959). It was based upon observations of retarded readers and beginning readers, but also upon analyses of the educational material with which pupils worked. The word 'rebus-reading' refers to elementary guessing reading, where the pupil reads each word separately without being aware of the whole.

When such a pupil is observed, it will be noticed that he recognizes some or single words, guesses others, tries to spell or sound still other words. He partly guesses the meaning of other words or collocations of words by means of the accompanying illustrations.

It might be said that the pupil who rebus-reads has his whole attention concentrated on making out what is written. There is no energy left to apprehend or experience the content of what has been read. At this level of reading instruction pupils will generally be far more interested in the number of lines or pages they have read than in the content. When asked about the content, the pupils will often with reluctance and astonishment try to recall what they have read. But they will probably consider such a question a little irrelevant in relation to the fact that they really "have read" the entire page or the entire paragraph.

According to educational observations in other countries similar phenomena occur. Many of the pupils who learn to read early in their lives use a kind of rebus-reading in the beginning. They have their interest primarily fixed on reading itself as a goal, not as something concerning content. Reading in itself, as a goal and not as a means, is characteristic of rebus-readers.

Transition-Reading

With the methodology of reading described in this book pupils usually change their reading technique during a rather limited period from two to perhaps 18 months. Their reading slowly changes from rebus-reading to content-reading. Frequently the transition between the two can be rather long. In many cases transition-reading may

31

be characterized as an independent stage for the pupils in question. It may be characterized as such from the standpoints of reading form, pupils' choice of reading material and observed reading difficulties which occur in connection with a certain book or a specific kind of educational material.

The demarcation of this stage is also discussed in another section of the book (cf. fig. 2).

Content-
Reading

It can be expected that pupils can be located in at least three stages during their reading development: rebus-reading, transition-reading and content-reading. The majority of pupils will eventually read in content-reading form. In the methodology described in this book reading is not only one clearly defined ability. Reading covers several things. It may be possible to distinguish other stages in the development of reading for particular pupils.

When viewed more closely the concept of content-reading is very complex. What characterizes content-reading is that the reading process itself functions. The reader interprets while he is reading. The reader is able to listen, get involved and with increasing maturity take an interrogative and critical position towards what he has read.

Skills in content-reading are a prerequisite for useful study skills, which might be considered an independent stage somewhat different from reading.

The Content-
Reader as
Rebus-Reader

Even if a pupil has become a content-reader of regular texts which correspond to her maturity, potentialities and interests, this pupil is not necessarily a content-reader of more difficult texts. There is always an interaction between each individual's linguistic and cognitive abilities and a given text. There are also differences in the reader's momentary being in gear or not being in gear. Reading is part of the individual's functioning, but an

32

integrated part. It can be seen only in relation to the entire situation of the individual.

The generally skilled reader not only stops wordvise when dealing with a professional text within an unknown area. The words may be well known but the way the words are put together different. The meaning is hard to grasp. The otherwise skilled reader will then suddenly become a rebus-reader and show for instance the characteristic mumbling form of the rebus-reader. Even with well-known texts the content-reader may regress due to a variety of circumstances such as a stressful life situation, a headache or sullen mood.

When observing pupils diagnosed as reading retarded, their work in nearly all cases is characterized as rebus-reading. However, an intelligent reading retarded pupil will be able to study, but the pupil in question reads all his study material in a rebus-like way. This form of reading is extremely time consuming and also intellectually demanding. Therefore it might be of value in work with specifically retarded readers to aim more at a qualitative description of their reading than at a quantitative measurement of their reading. That they are retarded readers is rarely doubted by their teachers or themselves. Whether they are in grade seven or nine is of less significance compared with their wish for help. *Rebus-Reading – Also the Form of Reading of Retarded Readers*

Perhaps investigations focused on qualitative descriptions would be more directly profitable. Observations of pupils are becoming more usual and extensive with the increasing acceptance of classroom-observations. This has resulted in descriptions of teaching intentions and also actual happenings. Gradually what pupils are experiencing is also being described.

Another way of classifying reading other than in stages and form is in terms of various reading techniques such as scanning, skimming, close reading, etc. Most of these *Scanning, Skimming, etc.*

techniques are somewhat ambiguously defined by various researchers and methodologists. There are evident discrepancies in the descriptions from country to country. It may be said that classification according to reading techniques is reading seen from the tool side. The classifications described in the previous pages is reading seen from the pupil-side. In later chapters work with scanning and skimming will be described.

A Critical Remark on Instruction in Critical Reading

In this connection working on critical reading might be mentioned. Critical reading may be more or less subordinate to general intellectual development, knowledge based on experience, cognitive development, etc. In much teaching material addressing itself to children and in many teaching situations with children, critical reading is supposed to be trained. Now and then one gets the impression that what is trained is seeing the same aspects as the teaching material does, or having the same prejudices as the teacher has, rather than dealing with the reading process based on the pupil's independent development and independent personality.

Reading Instruction in Kindergarten?

While kindergarten is a place for children from 3 to about 6–7 years of age, the kindergarten class is for 6- to 71year-old children. (see also fig. 18, p. 148).

The kindergarten aims at giving children the possibility for a secure and stimulating life during a number of hours daily irrespective of their parents' greater or smaller educational insight. The kindergarten is a place where children meet the norms of the surrounding society in phase with their own development. The kindergarten aims at being a place where children assisted by adults in relation to other child age groups are taught to respect others and to create respect for themselves. Kindergarten should also be a playground for children and a workshop offering possibilities for manual training and experiences with things and fantasy. All this implies that a kinder-

34

garten is not considered a pre-school and does not work with what might be called pretraining in reading.

In the kindergarten class the forms of work of the kindergarten are continued, but the aims of school become more explicit. There is no reading instruction for children in the kindergarten class either. On the other hand, linguistic teaching aims exist.

Reading Instruction in Kindergarten Class?

A language is not developed in a social and emotional void. When children are going to learn reading, there must be a background of spoken language which is understood. This is something which is developed in whole situations, not only through pencil and paper activities. There is absolutely no formal teaching of reading and arithmetic in the kindergarten class. It is emphasized that the language must be heard, spoken and understood and a broad background developed. If not, the school would build on sand, and reading would become something unfunctional which could not be used for any purpose.

Mother tongue teaching at school must be something which runs parallel to – and not beside – the general linguistic development of the child.

Learning is not piling new materials on the top of others which are already present. It is a process which creates its own materials and integrates and models further what already exists.

The interest in school maturity tests has been rather limited during the years and now such tests are practically not used. It is considered more essential to have an interest in whether the school is mature for the children than whether the child is mature for the school. It is significant that no Danish school maturity test exists. An adjusted form of a Swedish test and a Norwegian test have been used, but these tests have now disappeared in practice.

Does Reading Maturity Exist?

Likewise it is characteristic that interest in reading

35

maturity has been limited. There has never been qualified work with reading maturity tests to any significant extent. This should be viewed in connection with the fact that in the early stages of education teacher observations are emphasized in preference to testing, as is the teachers' free choice of appropriate means and methods.

Problems with Individualization

When pupils come to school, they should all be taught wherever they stand and in a way which suits pupils and teachers best. This has been the official point of view. Individualization in teaching is emphasized, although how far this has succeeded might be questioned. Apparently many teachers have used the provisional solution of a very slow learning including very slow reading learning during the first school years. This is hardly a satisfactory solution in all situations. This attitude is based on a fundamental viewpoint of the old official educational guide. "In all education of beginners it is necessary to keep in mind that heavy demands on the pupil may well reduce the benefit of education in the long run". (The Ministry of Education, 1961). In living up to this viewpoint, maybe even to a higher degree than necessary in many cases, it is not unusual that a great number of pupils do not learn reading until an age of 10 years.

The Viewpoint on Method of Reading

In preference to being interested in the cultivation of methods of instruction, interest has been directed towards the entire educational situation of the child. The official attitude is that neither a spelling method, nor a phonetic method, nor a look-say method, nor other so-called methods are viewed as the only method.

It is a common trait that *the method* of reading instruction is viewed with much distrust as well. It is directly denied that there exists, or that it might be possible to establish, one method which is good in itself and which is useful in all situations (Jansen, 1968). Method imperialism has never fallen on fertile soil in reading instruction in Denmark as described in this book.

In spite of this official and practiced rejection of one single method, certain characteristics of reading instruction can be identified.

Reading Instruction for 6- to 8-Year-Old Children

During the first months of school there is quite intensive work with rather few words. These words are supported by a systematic learning of letters. At the same time rebus-reading is developed through a high degree of integration between pictures and text.

Gradually, emphasis is placed on pupils being able to read the most simple easy reading booklets and tiny books. The pupil is given the opportunity to jointly select further training material. In most cases a systematic but not rigid application of one of several possible basal reading programs is attempted. Individualization is fostered by a generous application of supplemental educational material.

The introductory phase is characterized by many games of words and letters and exercises with letter boxes, and getting acquainted with books, pamphlets, etc. Motor learning of letters is supported by writing them. This is not considered a pre-exercise in handwriting but primarily support for learning to read. Conversation is cultivated systematically, probably with the same result as in most countries. The teacher is the one who is most skilled and remains most skilled in speaking, perhaps because she is the one who speaks most.

Introductory Phase

During the first two or three years of school split half-classes allow the teacher to work with half of the class during a large number of the lessons in the mother tongue language. This has had great significance as regards reading instruction. It should also be mentioned that in

Administrative Characteristics

the Danish language 'the teacher' is referred to as " ... he". In fact, half of the teachers in this country are male. Even if the percentage of female teachers is considerably higher than male in the youngest classes, it is still possible for almost all pupils to have male as well as female teachers during their first years of schooling. Perhaps more as a matter of curiosity it can be mentioned that mathematics teachers often are a "he" while Danish teachers – mother tongue teachers – often are a "she".

After the
Introductory
Phase

Between six months to one year after the start of instruction, basal readers become the main educational material. Parallel to the work with the basal reader, individualized silent reading comes in. During the second year of schooling the textbook is as a rule the chief teaching material. It should be noted that the central point of this work is the presentation of and working through the textbook and not its use in tests and examination. In this period topics such as training in small words and exercises of dividing into syllables are emphasized. However, it is essential that the pupils maintain a positive relationship to learning and that they have faith that they can learn to read.

Reading
Associated with
Solution
of Tasks

Reading with solution of tasks is characteristic for the last part of the first and second years of school. The pupils can work rather extensively with reading, but before they get tired of the reading process, they can start working on what they have read. For instance, they can answer questions and perform small tasks in relation to the text. The central purpose of this activity is of course that independent reading and reading with solution of tasks point towards later use of reading material for studying.

Reading
Instruction for ...

It should be recognized that there are limitations to the idea of class levels in reading as made in these margins:

38

There are great differences between the pupils in a single class as well as between classes. There are differences between schools which will often have pupils from dissimilar environments.

With a certain hesitation it might be said that the teaching of reading to the 8- to 10-year-olds involves the pupils selecting an essential part of their reading material and reading a great deal. It is a question of letting them read a lot independently. The pupils will choose the more difficult material as they can manage it. On this point children do not differ from adults. Also like adults, it often seems that some pupils choose much too difficult prestige kind of books in preference to easy ones.

Again there are pupil differences, some of which have their origin in personality structures. The timid pupil chooses another way than the self-confident pupil. The pupil who intends to impress his surroundings chooses another way than the shy one.

An important prerequisite for the reading instruction described here is that there is much material available in the classroom. Instruction is varied in duration and level of difficulty. Pupils work with easy, often self-chosen literature and also with reading with solution of tasks. This latter kind of reading will often be on more difficult materials. It is merely a forerunner of reading technique exercises in a later phase. Often reading with solution of tasks is most satisfactory intellectually to some pupils. This is not always the case with the somewhat thinner texts they can read themselves.

Not infrequently some of the pupils need easy non-fiction reading. Here a factor enters which blocks off such work. There are not enough books (especially non-fiction) which meet both the intellectual and interest level of the pupils and their reading ability. Television and magazines provide many pupils with subject matter knowledge largely in picture form. This places heavy demands on the technical development of books useful to

39

readers who are rather weak in reading ability. Such books are available in much too small numbers. Non-fiction books which coordinate intellectual and linguistic levels with interest are somewhat scarce. Therefore many pupils on this level must be content with more casual non-fiction and with fiction which is designed for intellectually weaker pupils. In practice, therefore, reading with solution of tasks will be not only an excellent situation of work but often the most meaningful situation in which these pupils can be placed as far as reading is concerned.

Reading Instruction for 10- to 12-Year-Old Pupils

On this level pupils start choosing ordinary children's books. They also occasionally read books for adults, especially books which appeal to the pupil because of their topics. The question is whether such adult materials should be introduced earlier like it is often done in German- and French-speaking countries – it is also seen occasionally in Sweden and in English-speaking countries. On the other hand one might wonder whether such materials are introduced too early in those countries?

The Results of This Educational Approach

What may especially characterize the results of this educational approach is the large range of the pupils in a class. Some pupils have become book-eaters at the same time that others still work with reading with solution of tasks and a few pupils are still rebus-readers.

However, a great number of books are lent to children – as indicated in figure 19, App. B in this book.

It is also known that children read children's classics. This raises the question: To which extent do children in all these countries read classics? In Denmark all children read *some* classics, and some children read quite many classical texts; but in this country this advanced reading is put into action relatively late. One may choose to emphasize the final result, as the supporters of the method described here do; or one may choose to emphasize that it

40

should be possible for the pupils, or at least part of them, to work with relatively advanced reading material at the earliest possible age.

Before this stage, instructional work has been concerned with key words and with reading simple graphic pictures. Some attempts have been made with critical reading and accurate reading in various versions. Between the ages of 11–13, pupils generally have the reading and intellectual prerequisites for beginning work in scanning. A few pupils are also able to work with skimming.

Reading Instruction for 11- to 13-Year-Old Pupils

From about the third year of school the teacher occasionally has compared the pupil's reading speed (slow or quick reading) with the pupil's reading accuracy (few or many errors). On this basis it is possible to place a pupil in one of four groups as indicated in figure 1. The method of reading instruction will vary for each group.

"Silent reading with control"		
number of errors reading speed ↓ ———→	few errors	many errors
quick reading	①	②
slow reading	③	④

Figure 1

The pupils in group 1 should be allowed to choose still more difficult reading material. For these pupils it is probably the time when writing the language might be trained more than previously. These pupils should also gradually start training in more advanced reading techniques. If their general intellectual development permits, they should deal with texts which are more demanding as far as learning is concerned.

The pupils in group 2 are overly conscientious, often

personally insecure. They should be encouraged to break the habit of reading every single word on every single page. It may be possible for some in the seventh year of school to start elementary systematic training in reading speed.

In group 3 are the too careless readers. They are often pupils whose entire form of work is marked by much looseness or by a supercilious attitude towards work. These pupils should work often in reading with control questions. They often derive benefit from working again with reading with solution of tasks. This is adapted to their higher degree of maturity and intellectual development.

In group 4 are the reading retarded pupils and others who need work with easy books and who need much reading. These often specially instructed pupils are discussed in the next chapter.

Reading For 13- to 16-Year-Old Pupils

After the sixth to seventh year of school the teaching of the mother tongue language is divided into several departments. Real reading instruction is only one of these, which should be relatively modest if the previous reading instruction has been fairly systematic. Still, continued reading instruction is necessary. Omitting such instruction would be limiting the possibilities of many pupils to really learn to read. Occasionally they are just getting started seriously. More extensive reading skills training is described in the following chapters and will not be discussed here. However, it should be mentioned that the amount of more extensive reading training described in this book is disproportionately larger than the actual time spent on it.

Furthermore, mother tongue instruction now consists of more traditional teaching of literature. Previous work with children's books, some anthologies and textbook anthologies has provided the basis for the teaching of literature. This sort of work with literature can hardly be distinguished from the work with literature well known

42

in many other places. This will not be investigated in this book.

– – –

The work with cultural heritage has been dealt with first through reading textbooks and eventually through certain special traditional books. In mother tongue teaching of the last few decades this has become a less significant activity, perhaps as a reaction to the importance previously placed on this kind of material, or as a consequence of the internationalization of much education. The latest trends consist of a limited sampling of a few classical topics and texts from the past. Here as well there seems to be international similarities. A search into the past is observed in many countries following a violent expansion of interest in the present time. The concern with this phenomenon may not be the alternation between the present and the past but the constantly lacking trait of systematic work with contents pointing towards the future.

Traditionally, the teacher who taught the mother tongue language was also the classroom teacher. It has been usual that those pupils who started in one class had the same teacher not for one or two years but either for two-three years or, by far the most usual, for five years. During the last few decades the period in which the classroom teacher has her pupils has grown longer. Now it is normal that the classroom teacher has pupils for seven years and in a great deal of cases for 9 or 10 years. At the present time in 90 percent of all cases the mother tongue teacher is also the classroom teacher (Jansen, 1973). This means that a great concentrated responsibility for a pupil's education is placed on one single teacher.

However, it should be stressed that the pupils of a class do not have one teacher only. They always have

The Classroom Teacher Is the Teacher of the Mother Tongue Language

43

two or more often three or more teachers. Pupils have their classroom teacher for Danish and religion and probably one or two other subjects. They have another teacher for mathematics and probably other subjects. As class grade level advances, the classroom teacher instructs the pupils in Danish and religion. Often this teacher later on teaches social studies and less frequently science. As the pupil advances, more teachers come into the picture.

The fact that the mother tongue teacher is also the classroom teacher may have many advantages of a social-educational kind. However, this strains the more professional aspect of the education particularly in terms of time that is available. But the fact that one teacher follows a class all the way through school, or large parts of it, provides a rather high degree of behavioral stability in school.

However, it must be recognized that the mother tongue as a vulnerable area of learning in some cases is strained by the large amount of extra curricular work which a classroom teacher does.

A new Education Act furthermore allocates all classes one weekly lesson to cover to some extent the classroom teacher's social pedagogic work and other social tasks. This is hardly sufficient time for the above classroom teacher functions, but the establishment of this "lesson of the class" must be considered fundamentally important.

Other Teachers It may be of interest that instruction in the first foreign language, English, is compulsory from the fifth year of school. The teacher of foreign languages is rarely the teacher of the mother tongue or mathematics for the same class. The other foreign language, German, is compulsory for all pupils from the seventh year of school. A third foreign language, French, is only taught during the 10th year of school and is elective.

44

Instruction in Latin is voluntary for the pupils 15 years old (ninth year of school). It is rather rudimentary and somewhat of a curiosity.

Most of the pupils master English rather well. The profit from German is probably very modest for a few pupils and hardly completely satisfactory for most of the pupils, although the understanding of German is rather good. The gain from the third foreign language, French, is problematic.

The teachers of art, music and gymnastics, etc. are usually specialists. It is rarely the classroom teacher who teaches these subjects in her class after the first two years.

The description of mother tongue instruction has concentrated on reading. Other aspects of the mother tongue are also taught. The spoken language is probably taught too casually and too little.

Other Aspects of Mother Tongue Instruction

The written language is also taught. Previously instruction in correct spelling was very much emphasized. This was an influence from German and Middle-European teaching. The changes which took place between 1940–45 in the Danish schools (Jansen, 1966), slowly led to a greater emphasis on creative writing and independently written composition.

If the various sub-aspects of mother tongue teaching are viewed together, differences between pupils have increased during the last few decades.

If this is the effect of the Danish idea of equality through education it must be said that it differs quite a lot from the intentions: During school a higher percentage of the pupils actually acquire more knowledge than they did earlier. They go further in their own development. On the other hand, other pupils take longer to reach the level of attainment that they would have been able to reach earlier. The group of pupils reaching higher than before is growing through the grades and is

45

also considerably higher than the group of pupils reaching lower levels than before (Jansen & Glæsel, 1977).

This so-called "two-hunched distribution" up through the grades is quite remarkable, the more so as neither of its extremes are easily characterized.

In the mother tongue teaching there are too many boys in the lower end, but there are also girls. There are too many pupils from the so-called socioeconomically badly situated families, but definitely also pupils from other socioeconomic groups – just as there are pupils from all groups, and that to quite a large extent, in the total distribution.

The only thing that seems to characterize the pupils not scoring well is a general tendency to refrain from penetrating into problems that seem difficult to them.

Three Aspects of the Teaching Materials

In analyzing teaching materials (Jansen, 1969) and especially in viewing these teaching materials in relation to each pupil's work, different reactions have been observed in various groups of pupils. These have involved three aspects which characterize the teaching materials:

1. typographical aspects – letter form design, layout, etc.; i. e. the entire visual appearance of the teaching material;

2. linguistic aspects; i. e. the linguistic appearance of the texts used;

3. content aspects – of central importance in most cases.

Figure 2 attempts to show the reading development in relation to the evaluation criterion of the text used. It appears that the ciphers 3, 5 and 7 of each single step seem to be the most important.

On Typography and Legibility

There have been many studies on the significance of typographical factors in the legibility of texts from the many German studies around the turn of the century to

46

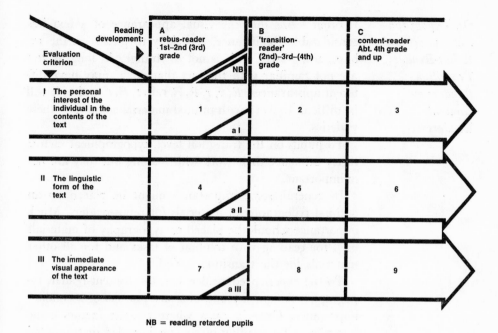

NB = reading retarded pupils

Figure 2

the many studies in English, especially American. Current studies are often related to problems concerning advertising technique. Concerning these typographical studies, it appears as if the usual is what is read best by most pupils. However, it is not sufficient to examine typography. It should be kept in mind that it is a question of the entire immediate appearance of a text. In this is included besides typography design, layout, colors, etc. This should also be viewed in relation to the possibilities of each group of pupils. If this holistic view is maintained, the matter may not be as confusing as it is often described in typographic research (Jansen, 1977).

*On Typograph-
ical Factors and
Rebus-Readers,
Transition-
Readers and
Content-
Readers*

It often seems that the visual appearance of a text has considerable significance, especially to pupils on the rebus-reading level. This is not so strange. As long as you are not familiar with the fact that an 'r' may have different appearances, R, r, r, R, R, r, R, r, *R, r* and R, it will be difficult to work with printed material containing these varieties.

To pupils on the transition level, typographical factors rarely influence their work with reading but they are not unimportant.

In general, some importance might be placed on an optimal typography of materials for rebus-readers. Much importance schould be placed on typography of materials used for reading with solution of tasks and for all other materials for the transition period.

To the experienced reader, i. e. the content-reader, typography, design, lay out, etc., are matters of secondary importance. Only in cases where specific factors come into play is the reading of content impeded or promoted by a special typography. However, experienced readers are not always content-readers. The experienced reader occasionally, for instance when tired, may be confronted with a very difficult text. He may be confronted with a text which is of great importance or be diverted by the complex visual appearance of the text in question.

*On Linguistic
Factors and
Rebus-Readers,
Transition-
Readers and
Content-
Readers*

The language of a text for rebus-readers must be very simple. Occasionally it may be so simple that it is almost drained of content. Language is about the greatest obstacle for a pupil's acquistion of a text on this level.

For pupils on the transition reading level, it often appears that linguistic appearance is of essential importance. As mentioned previously, typography is somewhat essential on this level, although still not central. The content is definitely important and the older and more conscious of content the pupil becomes, the greater weight content will carry, whether the pupil is a rebus-reader or transition-reader. From observation of the reading of many pupils, a pupil in the transition-reading stage often independently tackles a linguistically comprehensible text but rejects the linguistically difficult text. It appears that there is a lack of capacity in the transition-reader to work with linguistically difficult material. This pupil will try to acquire the content. When she does not succeed, it will often be due to a linguistically difficult array of the content. This directly blocks off comprehension.

It is possible to identify two relatively observable groups of pupils who are retarded readers: 1) the very heavily reading retarded, who will often be mainly visually retarded readers, and 2) the intellectually retarded, backward, pupils. It appears that they are impeded by different linguistic factors. *Two Different Groups of Reading Retarded*

The very heavily visually retarded pupil seems to be blocked when confronted with long words. This may be viewed in relation to an earlier stage where he is impeded by too small a space between each word compared with the space between the lines and letters.

In contrast, the backward pupil is blocked by long sentences. However, it may be difficult to decide whether it is also the content of the text which blocks in these cases. A content difficult text is often identical with a text with long sentences. During the work in developing norms for measuring readability (Jakobsen, 1970 (a) and 1975), based on Swedish studies (Björnsson, 1968), it appeared that the backward reader was specifically impeded by long sentences.

It should be emphasized that it is not a question of a mainly visually retarded reader, a backward reader or an ordinary reader. There are innumerable intermediate stages between these groups of readers. The same reader will function differently in different situations according to the general situation: personal, usual energy or the *Many Stages among Readers* contrary, the concrete or abstract content of the text, the purpose of reading, etc. Even keeping the above-mentioned reservations in mind, it is still necessary to be attentive to the linguistic appearance of a text, particularly with pupils from around 8½ years of age to about 10–11 years of age. The literature especially developed for the reading retarded, in which linguistic considerations have been emphasized, has also been successful with the previously mentioned age levels. There may be many reasons for this, but among others the linguistically difficult text has a blocking effect on the transition reader (Jansen, 1971 (a)).

On Content-Reading and Content

To the content-reader the content of a text is absolutely decisive. By far most people are content-readers, especially in a decidedly literary society such as the Danish one. But, once again, it should be emphasized that the competent adult content-reader will occasionally function on another level!

During the last few years much interest in content has developed. A great deal of literature on this topic has emerged in other countries (Zimet, Blom and many others). Within Scandinavia the topic has been much discussed. In Appendix C a content analysis of Danish textbooks most commonly used for reading instruction is presented.

The road to wisdom? - Well, it's plain
and simple to express:
Err and err and err again
but less and less and less.

3.

Remedial instruction in reading

Regarding remedial instruction in Denmark one should refer to *Reading Disabilities* (Tarnopol, 1976) which gives up-to-date information on this kind of education and attempts to place it in a wider educational context. For a description of the attitude behind this form of education and of the conditions necessary for its accomplishment, one should refer to Jansen, Ahm, Jensen and Leerskov (1970).

There is no precise information on how many pupils receive remedial instruction for reading retardation during their school years between the age of 7 and 16. A prevalence of about five percent is estimated, i. e. one out of 20 pupils at any given time receive remedial teaching. This corresponds to an incidence of about 20 percent, i. e. the probability is one out of five that a certain pupil in his entire school life will receive some sort of remedial teaching sooner or later.

How Many Receive Remedial Teaching in Reading

The two key persons dealing with remedial instruction issues are the classroom teacher and the school psychologist. A recommendation of a pupil for remedial instruction in reading will always start with the classroom teacher. She can describe the problems of the pupil as they are observed now and as they have also been observed during the previous years. It should be noted again that the classroom teacher usually follows her class for quite a number of years. The classroom teacher amplifies the description by noting how the pupil reacted to previous treatment(s) carried out in the class and by gathering information from the parents.

The school psychologist follows this up by describing the pupil's symptoms from other points of view: from observation in the class, interviews and tests.

A key factor in the diagnostic procedure is the child's way of functioning at school, viewed as a whole. It is important to consider whether the pupil has a teacher who is especially matched or mismatched with the pupil in question, whether his classmates have favorable or unfavorable effects, whether the pupil has close friends in the class or lacks such friends, etc.

In evaluating facilities for the reading and linguistically retarded, there is a tradition in professional literature to look at some facilities and not at others.

It may also be reasonable to look at other factors such as teachers' wages. They are in general relatively high in Denmark. Furthermore the teacher in special education has the advantage that his or her number of weekly lessons is somewhat reduced in comparison with that of the teacher in ordinary classes.

Today a little more than 10 percent of the sum of teachers' wages in Denmark are used in the entire remedial teaching system.

Furthermore, all teachers are educated as such, school

buildings in general are well equipped, and considerable book and educational materials are available for retarded readers (cf. Appendix B). During the last few years there has been a slight tendency to supplement book materials with electronic and mechanical learning apparatus. However, in a very small language area (Danish) the learning apparatus will remain unused most of the time due to the lack of software. Perhaps also for that reason a teacher relies on books and games designed for learning.

School psychologists should also be counted among the facilities, not only in their testing and diagnostic function, but also for directly following the remedial instruction. There is one school psychologist for 1,000–2,000 pupils. The average class size is rather small (see figure 3). There is also the classroom teacher tradition. This tradition has proved quite effective in its social-educational function.

The work is based primarily upon trying to compensate for pupil weaknesses by improving their strengths.

Principles of Remedial Instruction in Reading

The special education teacher tries to view the entire situation of the pupil. Persistent formal training is considered ineffective if practiced in isolation as is work based on creative interests only. It is essential to direct education towards an objective so that it becomes part of a whole. Work is based upon each child's or group of children's possibilities and potentialities. One rarely bases the work on an educational program scheduled beforehand. Something like teacher intuition directs the education.

These three principles: 1) compensating for weakness through strength, 2) training and work that is placed in the whole context of the child's life, and 3) procedures based on the child's actual possibilities and potentialities, form the basis of remedial instruction. These principles lead to a teacher attitude which does not allow the pupils to direct the work or the teacher to direct it alone. It might be said that the teacher listens to the pupils, but

53

she does not let them take charge of affairs. Guidance by materials and procedures is frequently used.

Many Methods within Special Instruction in Reading

Many methods have always been used in remedial instruction. They are often appropriately applied and occasionally less so in relation to the handicaps of pupils.

Many educational currents during the last few years have also made their way through special education in mother tongue language. This is true of the work with phonics, with words in color, with programmed instruction, with kinesthetic methods and with training in the spoken language. However, apart from a few enthusiastic supporters, hardly any have expected 'the great good method' to emerge (Jansen, 1968 (a)). Since the learning possibilities of the pupils are complex, it is generally held that one method cannot be the solution. Pupil difficulties are different. Consequently, the methods must be several, and they are often varied or mixed.

Environment as Therapeutic

This has led to an emphasis on environment, time and materials.

Environment include the child's total situation. This has also been mentioned with ordinary education. The emphasis on environment leads to a therapeutic attitude. Perhaps this should be seen as "the method". "The method" should be the positive emotional influence from the surroundings focused on remedial instruction. A remediation of functions takes place in a highly personal interaction between reading teacher and each pupil.

Time for Maturation and Emotional Unlocking

For some years it was usual to rely on the fact that the teacher could, or had to, wait for the child's maturation. Time was used to loosen emotionally locked situations which affect the possibilities for learning. Many have experienced that waiting for maturity did not lead to positive results in all cases. However, it may be beneficial for those pupils who are locked up emotionally.

One primarily counts on materials which can be accepted *Materials* emotionally and intellectually by the pupils. These are *Accepted* preferred to materials specifically constructed for certain *by Pupils* handicaps.

There are modifications in relation to pupils with obviously specific handicaps.

Among the group of pupils receiving special education *What is* the reading retarded are viewed as most successfully *Reading* adaptable to ordinary school environment. A common *Retardation?* view among teachers of reading retardation has probably contributed to this opinion.

Most teachers do not look upon reading retardation as a specifically limited and precisely defined handicap. The weak readers represent a long continuum where it is the resources of the society and the wishes and possibilities of the teachers which make the distinction between retarded and not retarded. Such a point of view will often lead to retarded readers being in the ordinary education system during economically prosperous periods. It is a practice that is supported by teachers who often want to keep remedial instruction numerically as small as possible for ideological reasons. Yet it should be said that in no previous period of time has remedial instruction increased so much. This has occurred during the present time when the abolition of special education and its integration in ordinary education has been discussed.

The strong development of remedial instruction in reading has been economically straining. However, it has indirectly been of benefit to other pupils. It has given the ordinary teacher knowledge about reading retardation, which in turn has contributed to the acceptance of this handicap by society. Effective remedial measures have worked in the same direction.

ON BEING ONESELF

Good-resolution grook

If virtue
can't be mine alone
at least my faults
can be my own.

4.

Individualization and pupil differences

It is a basic fact that people differ. These differences apply to all parts of the development of a child. They are certainly not smaller in the areas which are important for the child's development and learning at school. Pupils are different in personality structure, interests, acquired abilities and knowledge.

Pupils Differ – a Problem for Education

These differences present a problem for education because many pupils have to be taught by the same teacher at the same time. The pupils' benefit from their education

56

is highly dependent on how extensively these conditions are considered.

In many cases differences between pupils are so large that not all pupils in a group or a class aim at the same educational objectives. Individualization of education becomes necessary since pupils have different educational goals.

However, even when pupils work towards the same goals, they follow different paths to reach them. Again, individualization is necessary. In this case the education must be planned in a way that offers pupils different ways in their daily work.

Pupils have always been different, and consequently, their possibilities for benefiting from a given education have been different. There are several reasons why this is now acknowledged as a problem, and why the demand for individualization has been increasing during recent years.

The Increasing Demand for Individualization

First of all, individual psychology may have resulted in increasing attention to differences rather than similarities between human beings. This increasing consciousness of the individual may have contributed to the demand for individualization in education.

Moreover, economic and social development of recent decades has effected a change in the social-educational attitude. It has given rise to a heavier demand for a democratization of educational systems. It is a more widespread expectation that school is responsible for the development and acquisition of knowledge of each pupil.

School is no longer viewed as an institution whose function is merely education in the sense of passing on information. Today the aim of the school is more that each single pupil should develop his or her individual potentials to a maximum, whatever their further qualifications may be. This is a sign of the democratization of education.

If schools must endeavor to meet this objective, and

57

nearly all political parties in Denmark agree in this, the individual touch must be emphasized far more. Therefore a series of arrangements which take into account individual differences of pupils has to be started. That is why the individualization has been most intensely emphasized during recent years in the Scandinavian countries.

Two Different Approaches to Individualization

Two different approaches may be observed in the many suggestions for solution of the need to individualize education:

One form is the streaming of pupils into various schools or classes. When this way of differentation is used, repeating will also be used frequently. Such forms are characterized by organizational arrangements that adapt the pupils to the education foundation already laid down. The pupils are placed in the best possible fit across the fan of lines and classes which have been established. This form of individualization is not used anymore in the Scandinavian countries. All Scandinavian countries have a nongraded school for nine (or ten) years, and on the whole repeating is not used.

The other form is to consider those pupils who started school together as one group trying to adapt education to the different pupils. This adaptation must take place within the frame of the class or the year in school. Here education may be compared to a fan made broad enough to cover all pupils.

This latter approach is far the most difficult to realize. It demands that a series of other prerequisites are met. These may be described as a series of different procedures on different levels within everyday education. They will be distinguished as endeavors within the levels of 1) organization, 2) teaching methods and 3) learning materials. Finally, how these three levels have been employed in practice will be described in a series of reading instruction programs for young people and adults.

58

Organization of teaching refers to the decision on which teachers teach which groups of students which subjects. Important questions to be answered are:

How are the pupils to be divided in groups?

Are homogeneous or heterogeneous groups to be formed?

Should the groups be permanent, perhaps for many years, or should the groups change?

Organizational Problems

At the same time as the Danish elementary school was confronted with the increasing demand of meeting the individual needs of each pupil, it also had to meet a political demand that this could not be done by streaming. For social-political reasons, elementary school in Denmark during the last twenty years has moved towards a non-graded school. As many pupils as possible are kept together in the same class for a long time. Today Denmark, like the other Scandinavian countries, has a nine-year non-graded school where all pupils starting together in a first class are kept together in the same class for the entire period. In this respect the Danish elementary school differs from elementary schools in several other countries in that the problem of individualized teaching is increased. Therefore, it is of interest to look at the educational ideology and organizational conditions concerning individualization.

The Development in Denmark

Many people believe that the most essential condition for carrying through individualized teaching is that there should be few pupils in the classes. This basic point of view has influenced teaching in Denmark for many years. The Danish school for many years has worked on a reduction of the general class size. Today class size is smaller than in most other countries.

Small Classes

From figure 3 it can be seen that the average class size in the Danish elementary school is approximately 19,7

59

Percent of classes   **Elementary Schools**

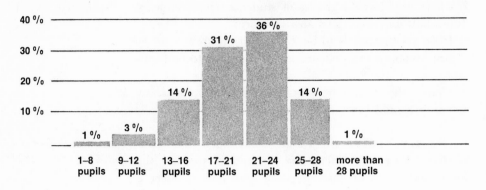

	1–8 pupils	9–12 pupils	13–16 pupils	17–21 pupils	21–24 pupils	25–28 pupils	more than 28 pupils
	1 %	3 %	14 %	31 %	36 %	14 %	1 %

Percent of classes   **Secondary Schools**

	1–8 pupils	9–12 pupils	13–16 pupils	17–21 pupils	21–24 pupils	25–28 pupils	more than 28 pupils
	1 %	8 %	29 %	33 %	23 %	5 %	1 %

Average Class Size

6– 7 years old	20.8
7– 8 years old	20.3
8– 9 years old	20.1
9–10 years old	20.1
10–11 years old	20.5
11–12 years old	20.3
12–13 years old	20.5
13–14 years old	19.5
14–15 years old	17.9
15–16 years old	16.1

Figure 3

pupils. There are classes with a considerably smaller number of pupils than the average. This is particularly found in rural districts where the school system has resisted centralization. On the other hand there are no classes with numbers of pupils as large as those reported from schools in many other countries. The Danish education law has fixed a maximum of 28 pupils. This means that a class has to be divided if the number of pupils exceeds 28.

In addition to the generally low class size, split half classes have been established within certain subjects and on some class levels. The class is divided into two groups who are taught separately for a number of lessons – the so-called split half classes. During these lessons only half of the pupils in the class are present. Half the class has the same teacher and the same subject. The other half gets the same instruction, only at another time. *Split Half Classes*

Split half classes are used in elementary instruction of reading and mathematics. They are also used later in the two compulsory foreign languages (English and German), but only during the first year of instruction. The number of split half class lessons varies from one class level to the other. They make up approximately five percent of all lessons.

The split half classes represent an organizational change, the aim of which is to avoid dividing the pupils according to achievement in order to get more homogeneous educational groups. On the contrary, it is the intention that this change in the number of pupils should encourage the teacher to teach individually. Educational research has shown that this arrangement has actually had the intended effect (Poul Erik Jensen, 1973). It is of general interest because most research on class size has shown that class size has no effect on teaching. A contribution to this effect has been that this organizational change has been followed by the development of educational materials and methods within the elementary level. The arrangement also prevents the teacher from continuing with total class instruction since only half the class is present.

Teacher Qualifications

Heavy demands are made on the qualifications of teachers when daily instruction is organized around the possibilities of each pupil. It is essential to consider where teachers are drawn from and how they are educated. To obtain a permanent appointment within elementary school, one should have an authorized education at the Teachers' Training College. This lasts four years after the completion of high school graduation. The schools mainly employ personnel with this education. It should be added that a very large number of teachers attend in-service training. Approximately 20 percent of the teachers attend in-service training courses every year. It is also necessary that teachers set aside time for preparation and planning of instruction. Thus a teacher in elementary school or secondary school instructs 27 lessons of 45 minutes each per week. But she or he gets paid for 40 hours of work, just like other employees.

Teaching Methods and Individualization

Individualization is not one special teaching method or one special way of organizing education. There are many teaching methods which provide more or less individualization. The crucial point is to what extent they are able to meet the differences of pupils. In estimating whether educational methods individualize, one should consider whether they fulfill various criteria.

One criterion is that the pupils work separately and independently.

Another criterion is that the pupils work with different materials and activities when working individually. It is not individualization if pupils are doing the same thing while working individually.

A third criterion is that various materials and activities

correspond with and are adapted to the differences of the pupils.

For a number of years an effort has been made to place an increasing part of the pupils' reading training in individual work. Through current research, in which forms of instruction at school have been studied through classroom observations (Jansen & Kreiner Møller, 1971, Jensen, 1973), it is possible to get an impression of how far the emphasis on individual work has developed in the Danish school.

Individualization in Elementary Schools

It appears from figure 4 that the pupils work individually during 37.3 percent of the entire time of instruction. This corresponds to the time spent on entire class instruction. This is far more time spent on individual work than what appears from classroom observation in most other countries.

Reading instruction should be based on pupils reading texts at a level of difficulty corresponding to their reading ability. How can instruction and educational materials be adapted to the background of each pupil? In Denmark a reading test or some other test is very rarely the basis of adapting educational materials to the pupil differences. Only a few reading tests exist and are used in school. In practice they are hardly ever used to determine daily reading instruction.

Pupil Motivation and Interest Is Central

Rather the pupils themselves choose their materials for independent reading. Consequently, it is often the pupil's motivation and interest which decides his choice of materials and his work. The materials are often supplemented by some teacher guidance which is influenced by intuitive understanding. It is only to a small extent determined by diagnosis from tests and systematic observations.

Reliance upon the motivation and interest of the pupil

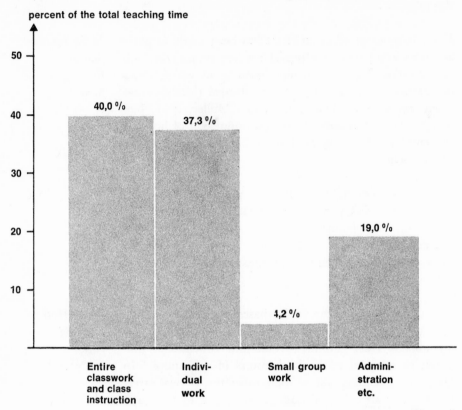

Forms of Instruction in a Class of Pupils between Eight and Nine Years of Age

percent of the total teaching time

Figure 4

to such an extent is based on a belief that those potentials of importance for the pupil's learning will be expressed in these ways. A pupil rarely chooses a book which is far above his reading ability, at least not for a long period of time. It is just as rare for a pupil to select reading material so simple that it does not provoke continued development of his reading ability.

A diagnosis can be deduced from the pupil's own choice of materials and forms of work. It is the pupil's diagnosis and is used to a certain extent.

64

The previously mentioned individualization cannot be practiced without a reasonably wide variety of educational materials. Materials should not only exist but pupils should also have direct access to them during daily instruction. Therefore, a school library is compulsory in all elementary schools. This is presumably the background for the large use of books from children's libraries and school libraries (cf. Appendix B, p. 152). Without a large supply and consumption of educational materials, individualization will not have reasonable possibilities at all.

Individualization and Teaching Materials

Since pupils choose their own educational materials, the design of the materials becomes important. It is necessary that the materials are spontaneously inviting and developed not only for teachers but also for pupils. The pupils must have a basis for selection. They should be able to evaluate the materials according to design, layout, typography, illustrations, etc., beforehand and not after they have worked with the materials.

The Design of Materials

Moreover, relatively few systematically designed materials are used within mother tongue instruction except at the beginning instruction. This applies to the educational materials as well as to the educational methods. For instance, only the first year's instruction is systematic enough to talk about methods of learning to read. After the first year of school the materials are not specifically aimed at a purpose. Danish educational materials are not designed exactly for this educational situation or that educational objective. Rather, they are constructed to be used in educational situations of different kinds. The material must contain several possibilities and grant more possibilities.

The same principle is found in some of the tasks in the educational materials. It is possible to distinguish between two types of tasks important for individualization.

On Formulation of Tasks

Directive tasks are those whose purpose is narrowly and specifically formulated. The form of the expected

65

Figure 5
Directive tasks demand specific skills which the pupil may have or not have.

answer will appear clearly. Often the pupil will be able to judge himself whether his solution is right or wrong. Tasks with only one correct answer are often of this type. The activities necessary for their solution are often presented unambiguously. There is just one correct way to the goal.

Open tasks are contrastingly different. Here the purpose of the tasks is so broadly formulated that the pupil can aim at various goals according to his or her potentials, interests and momentary capacity for working. The activity directions of these tasks are either few, or they may be of the type "you may for instance . . .". This broadness of activity directions ensures that different pupils may work with different activities started by the same task.

Directive tasks place emphasis on structuring the thinking and activity of the pupil through the task towards a specific goal. Thus they aim more specifically and they often demand specific skills which the pupil may or may not have. In this way the task is only relevant for a minority of the pupils in the class. In some pupils directive tasks may often raise feelings of failure because of insufficient background. Other pupils will feel they are wasting their time because they regard the tasks as too easy and offering no challenge.

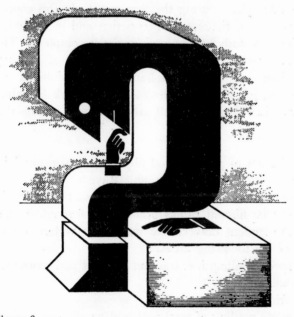

Figure 6
Open tasks are broadly formulated problems with many possible answers.

Open tasks, on the contrary, attach greater importance to the motivating and initiating aspect of the task. They do not direct the pupil along one track, and consequently, they will accommodate to differences between pupils as well.

<table>
<tr><td>An Example of
Individualiza-
tion in Reading
Courses</td><td>The Royal School of Librarianship provides education for librarians. This education lasts for four years after passing the high school examination. Every year 200 first year students are offered voluntary courses in reading skills training. More than half the students enroll. The organization of this course is described because it shows one possible solution to the problem of individualization.</td></tr>
</table>

An Introductory Course

The background for this rather high percentage of enrollment is a nine-hour introductory course for all students which takes place during the first month. In this course, reading tests in fiction and non-fiction and in skimming are given. A study habit questionnaire is completed. The students are introduced to the psychology of reading, note-taking techniques, work habits, work inhibitions and motivation for studying. The method of work is mainly plenary discussion and small group problem-solving discussion.

*Individualiza-
tion of
Instructional
Objectives
in Reading
Skills Training*

The selection of instructional objectives are inspired by McDonald & Byrne (1958) and Raygor (1965). The leading point of view is that the student should be taught whatever he himself thinks needs to be learned. Therefore, the student may choose instruction within one or more of the following areas:

1) speed-reading, i. e. training in faster and more varied reading,

2) skimming,

3) study reading of textbooks and handbooks,

4) counseling with respect to study problems.

Classes are made up of students who have selected rough-

68

ly the same course objectives. During the course, teaching is adapted to each student's progress towards these objectives. With this type of organization it has been possible to consider individual differences to a high degree.

Some of the students receive individual instruction for one quarter of an hour per week. All training occurs outside this instruction, which is used for evaluation discussion and planning new training activities (cf. p. 97). Other students are taught in groups of four–twelve. They receive one – one and a half hours of group instruction a week. The decision regarding group or individual instruction is based on the wishes of the students. It is determined by the principle of adapting course organization to the students. This principle has been described by Spache (1964).

Individualizing Method and Duration

The duration of the course is decided by the individual student; the average duration is about nine weeks but some students terminate earlier and others continue a little longer. In courses of fixed duration it has been noted that about half the students find that the course is too long and the other half that it is too short.

The drop-out rate is usually less than ten percent in most courses. This low figure may be attributed to the principle of individualization.

REVELATION AT MIDNIGHT

Infinity's taken
by everyone
as a figure-of-eight
written sideways on.

But all of a sudden
I now apprehend
that eight is infinity
standing on end.

5.

What speed-reading is

*Development
in Speed-
Reading
in Denmark*

During the last few years it has become common to educate young people and adults to improve the more technical aspects of their reading ability. This is important for effective work and learning. Some Danish schools have introduced a type of speed-reading from about 14 years of age. Short speed-reading courses for adults are also becoming more common although they are not as extensive as in the United States. The Danish television has programmed complete courses in speed-reading as part of television education for adults. There have also been television courses for schools (cf. Appendix D, p. 164ff).

The methodology used in these courses, and in most speed-reading courses in Denmark, differs considerably from courses in other countries. This is due to a different psychological conception of reading itself and how reading ability can be improved.

Psychological explanations are never the last word. It is possible to refer to circumstances associated with phenomena which require explanation, but these circumstances may not necessarily be causative. As an example, unsuccessful marriages might be considered. How is it possible to explain how such marriages become unsuccessful? It is possible to find many circumstances associated with these marriages: the man or the woman is rarely at home; the interests of man and woman are different; their points of view as regards children are different; they do not feel like spending their spare time together, etc. But are these events really the causes of an unsuccessful marriage or are they the symptoms of it?

Psychological Explanations of Good Reading

Similarly, the explanations of reading ability include many characteristics associated with good readers: congruence between reading purpose and comprehension of content, effective responses, quick eye movements, few fixations per line, no lip movements, etc. However, are one or all of these characteristics really causes of good reading, or are they only symptoms and signs?

Teachers and psychologists often view the process of reading in different ways. There is a corresponding difference in their explanations of improved reading ability, and of the facts influential in reading ability. Psychologists often express what they consider to be causes and symptoms. Presumptions about causes for good and bad

The Influence of Explanations on Teaching

71

reading are usually implicit in their explanations and interpretations.

It is important what explanations are used and what circumstances are considered causes. These circumstances influence teaching methodology. *When the psychologist attempts to explain what is happening in a person learning to read, the teacher will step in exactly at these points.* Furthermore the influence on teaching is also seen when the psychologist has not used the circumstances as causes in an explanatory way, but has used them as descriptions of reading ability.

Three ways of viewing reading will be examined in the following. Each of them is considered inexpedient because they contain little guidance for teaching or lead to a restriction in teaching.

Reading as Determined by Visual Perception

Some reading psychologists consider reading as visual perception and have little interest in reading experience or in reading comprehension. They explain reading ability entirely as measurable physical aspects of perception. The influences of lighting, typography and length of lines on reading speed have been examined. It is remarkable that most of these studies show that these factors have a rather small influence on reading speed. An influence is especially noted with extremes and in readers with specific weak reading capacities.

When these reading psychologists and teachers explain why reading speed has increased, they refer to factors related to peripheral sense organs. The causes of improved reading ability are seen as less and shorter fixations, fewer regressions and less mumbling, lip movements and tongue movements. These phenomena are of course clearly defined and easily measured. But they are not very profound explanations. One is reminded of the man who explains that he can run faster because his legs move faster. A fact has been explained just by describing it in other words.

72

Today reading teachers and reading psychologists consider eye movements and accompanying movements of the voice expressions of reading ability. They are not seen as symptoms of a good or bad reader nor as the causes of reading ability. Yet many have taken these aspects as causes for good and bad reading.

This viewpoint has had an undesirable influence on teaching methodology. Some courses try to improve the reading ability of students by improving their eye movements and by eliminating lip movements and accompanying movements of the voice. This is an example of how reading teachers train functions which the psychologists have used as explanations. In our opinion this is rarely an expedient teaching practice.

The reading capacity of a person is often labeled "his reading ability". For instance it is said: "he has low reading ability" meaning he reads poorly. In this context the use of the concept reading ability, is reasonable because it is used descriptively only. *Reading as Determined by an Ability*

Now and then reading ability is used as an explanation. It is said: "he reads poorly because he has low reading ability." Here, reading ability is stated as a cause for poor reading. In the same way, improved reading is explained by improved reading ability. Such an explanation refers to an ability *which has no other appearance than exactly the one it was supposed to explain!*

Other reading researchers explain better reading capacity by reference to visual ability or perceptual ability. This means a person's ability for quick, precise and correct visual perception. Extensive research has attempted to demonstrate a relationship between reading ability and visual ability (Vernon, 1969). However, it has not been possible to find specific visual factors which correspond with reading ability. These concepts can be criticized in the same way as reading ability. It is not possible to

73

explain something just by referring to other phenomena which are unknown and unverifiable. Nevertheless these concepts are rather widespread and have had an influence on teaching methodology. Attempts have been made in many courses to improve reading ability by training of perception. This consists of discrimination exercises, differentiation between different figures, and tachistoscopic training which emphasizes the perception of certain words in the shortest time possible.

Whether these activities concern the process of reading cannot be determined. One cannot recommend that courses spend too much time for such exercises. They are not included in the speed-reading methodology described in this book.

Reading as Determined by Perceptual Span

Some reading researchers explain reading ability as a function of perceptual span. While reading, an individual fixates his eyes a number of times on a line. When for instance a person fixates five times within one line, he will see an area surrounding the point of fixation. This usually correspond to one fifth of the line at each fixation point. This area is called the perceptual span of the reader.

It can be ascertained that quick readers have fewer fixations per line than slow readers. Improved reading ability is explained by stating that the person has extended his perceptual span and uses a smaller number of fixations per line.

However, the perceptual span as such is not measurable. It is possible to record what the eye is directed towards. It is also possible to measure how many visual stimuli at a given moment affect the retina. This will most often be much more than the page at which teachers expect students to be looking.

One does not know how many visual stimuli form part of the central processing of the central nervous system and become visual experiences. This will naturally de-

74

pend upon which visual stimuli hit the retina, but it will also depend upon other things. If the perceptual span is measured by the tachistoscope, it will be quite different if the span is measured as figures, letters, single words or words in a meaningful context.

Secondly, it is easily demonstrated that visual stimuli outside 'the perceptual span' may interfere with the central processing and consequently become visual experiences. If for instance in a tachistoscopic experiment one makes a red spot far out at the edge of a word map, this spot will be experienced by the reader even though it is situated outside the so-called perceptual span. Even visual stimuli located peripherally in the retina have the possibility of joining the processing of visual stimuli.

Therefore perceptual span cannot be used as an explanation since it, too, refers to something unknown, and unverifiable. A reader cannot experience his perceptual span. It cannot be defined, recorded or measured in an unambiguous way. Perceptual span is a hypothetical construct that has been invented to explain reading but in fact has no existence. It is unfortunate that some reading teachers have been influenced by this concept. This results in reading in artificial teaching situations that are far from ordinary reading but aim at extending the presumed perceptual span.

Three ways of viewing reading have been described, each of which is too narrow in concepts. Therefore, they lead to a false restriction of the methodology of reading skills training. They are too narrow because they deal with the first part of the reading process only – how the printed letters become visual impressions for the reader and which aspects of the outer world have an influence on these impressions. These views neglect the last part of the reading process – how visual impressions are transformed into content, thought, and meaning. Reading is a complex process. In the broadest sense it is all that happens when

An Applicable Explanation

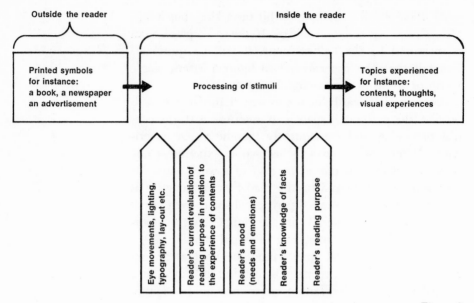

Figure 7

the reader sees some printed symbols (letters) and on this basis experiences content, thought, and meaning. Some of these aspects have been represented in the diagram of the reading process in figure 7.

Experiences Are Determined by the Process of Stimuli

The same physical stimuli are not always processed in the same way so that the final result is the same experience. The experience is not determined unambigously by the stimuli. From the psychology of perception it is known that an individual's needs and attitudes determine his experiences. Within the tradition of perceptual psychology much interest and work has been devoted to the processes between perceptual stimuli and experiences. These are called the processing of stimuli (Franz From, 1971).

Usually one has the illusion that the meaning lies in the text. This leads to the belief that the reader's job among

76

others is to understand this meaning. The content of the text is something which develops in the consciousness of the reader. The meaning or content is not presented unambiguously in the text. The visual stimuli do not become experiences until they are processed in the central nervous system of the reader. The text is an influence so ambiguous that many kinds of meaning can be experienced. Naively expressed it might be said that the text contains many meanings or much information.

The Experience of Meaning Is Determined by the Processing of Stimuli

Therefore, it is important to pay attention to the processing of stimuli connected with reading. It is most likely that the improvement of reading ability, which takes place during reading skills training, is due to a change in the processing of stimuli. This can explain why the teaching of literature can change the spontaneous experience of literature for the reader; why a book is experienced differently by different individuals; and why a book may be experienced quite differently the first and the second time it is read. It can be concluded that meaning does not lie in the text. It is contained in our experience, and this experience depends on the various factors which influence the processing of stimuli.

One of the products of the processing of stimuli is the experience of meaning. Another product is directing the way of reading such as eye movements and concurrent voice movements.

Processing of Stimuli Influences Ways of Reading

The Swedish researcher, Åke Edfeldt, examined concurrent voice movements during reading, and demonstrated that all readers have these movements when facing a text which is sufficiently difficult for them. It is obvious that concurrent voice movements arise whenever the reader finds it difficult to process the content of a text (Edfeldt, 1968). Thus voice movements are a product of the processing of stimuli.

The same phenomenon is likely true for regressions. When reading, one makes regressions now and then.

77

These regressions may go back to words that have been difficult to comprehend or to fit into the context of meaning. There is no conscious determination of regressions. We hardly ever know when we do them. Regressions arise, whenever there are difficulties with the processing of stimuli from the text.

The circular interaction of experience of content, eye and voice movements, visual impressions and processing of stimuli are demonstrated in figure 8.

Such facts are not always acknowledged within reading research. Within the psychology of perception it has been gradually accepted that perception is an active process. An interaction takes place between 1) stimulation of the sensory organs, 2) processing of these stimuli, 3) the central nervous system's regulation of the peripheral sensory organs which has the effect that 4) the stimulation of the sensory organs is changed. Physiologically this interaction between influence on the sensory organs and the central nervous system has been established.

Figure 8

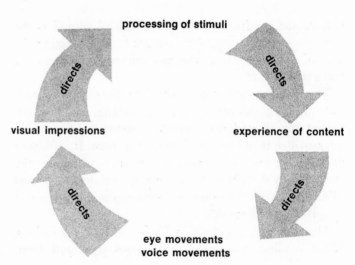

processing of stimuli

visual impressions

experience of content

eye movements
voice movements

The experience of content is determined by the processing of stimuli – yet how is that determined? The processing of stimuli depends on many factors within the text and within the reader. In figure 7 some of these factors are mentioned. The process is dependent on: *What Determines the Processing of Stimuli?*

– the reader's knowledge of what the text is dealing with;

– the amount and the content of the reading material;

– what the concepts mean to the reader;

– the reader's desire to read a certain kind of content;

– the reader's expectation as to what a given text says;

– the reader's purpose in reading the text.

Other factors probably have an influence on the processing of stimuli during reading. Research on reading has only been interested in these factors to a limited extent. It would be of interest to research as well as to practical teaching to examine whether a knowledge of the facts described in a text has an influence on reading speed. Shores (1968) has demonstrated that reading speed of children and adults is increased when the reader has a specific purpose for reading. When readers know what they should be looking for, they read far more quickly.

The intention or purpose of reading is of great significance for teaching methodology. *What is learned during a speed-reading course is to change the processing of stimuli during reading.* One learns to adapt the process so that the experience of meaning corresponds with the reading purpose. One reads the central contents, i. e. what is central to the reader at a given moment. Once this point has been grasped, one is able to increase reading speed. Then larger parts of the text will be perceived as being of less importance. *Speed-reading Involves Adaptation to Reading Purpose and Meaning*

The central point is a continuous evaluation of reading purpose in relation to reading experience. This evaluation depends on how trained each reader is in clarifying

79

reading purpose and experience of meaning. It is an extremely difficult task. These are not phenomena which can be observed and measured. It is a question of experiences which are difficult to describe in words even for the reader.

The Degree of Processing

There is an important aspect of reading purpose and reading experience which one must learn to describe and clarify. The text contains so many elements of content (information units) that it is impossible to experience all of them. Processing takes place during reading which consists of choosing the elements the reader has a need to experience. The reader's needs, expectations, attitudes, and purpose determine the elements that are processed and experienced, and those which are not processed.

It may be clarified by describing the process in the following way. The meaning of a text may have different clarity. It can be experienced as dim and vague or general. Reading about a person drinking wine with his food, one may experience the content of the text as:

1. his thirst, or
2. his thirst and the fact that he drinks, or
3. his thirst and the fact that he drinks wine, or
4. his thirst and the fact that he is actually drinking, or
5. his thirst and the fact that he is actually drinking the Chateauneuf du Pape mentioned in the text.

It is not a question of one kind of experience being incorrect. The experience has different specifications or degrees of processing. This degree of processing depends on many factors, reading speed being one. With greater reading speed the experience of meaning will often have less specification.

One gets a distinct impression of this phenomenon when skimming. The experience of reading becomes a less processed experience of totality. The reader does not feel that he lacks something or that there are holes, but the quality of experience is different. It is wider and more diffuse than from slow perusal. Afterwards the reader in describing his experience of meaning will often use words such as: "it was something on ...". This qualitative aspect of an experience is not only true for reading. It is present in all experiences. A more thorough description of this phenomenon may be found in Franz From (1971).

This fact has decisive significance for the methodology of reading training. If the reader wants to learn quicker and more varied reading, it is necessary that he recognizes both reading purpose and reading experience. He should be able to perform a continuous evaluation of the concordance/discordance between them.

In many studies where the effects of speed-reading courses are examined, the comprehension is controlled by successive questions. Comprehension, as already mentioned, is an experience. It is a complex experience of sequential thoughts which may be difficult to explain clearly. Control questions, for instance multiple-choice questions, provide a very poor estimation of this complex totality. For the same reason comprehension cannot be stated in percentages. It is also a flagrant simplification to maintain that comprehension is the same during slow and quick reading.

Evaluation of Speed-Reading

It is far more relevant to give a somewhat meticulous description of the experience of meaning at different reading speeds with different readers. Not until then will one know what changes have taken place during a course in speed-reading. Nor will it be possible to say anything meaningful about the difference between the good and the poor reader. Otherwise it will be possible to continue the discussion on how much reading speed can be increased without changing comprehension, without reaching a clarification in this discussion.

Summary

Reading and improvement in reading is clearly related to visual stimulation. Probably this aspect of reading is the least important. Reading is not a limited ability which can be trained in the same way as learning to type or to ride a bicycle.

Reading is a complex cognitive function in which the central aspect is the processing of stimuli taking place during the reading and leading to experiences and thoughts. Different ways of reading exist and each of them results in different experiences of meaning.

A reading course does not only mean working with improvement of the reading ability through increasing reading speed and preserving the reading experience. This is far too simplified. On the contrary, reading skills training is teaching the reader several ways of reading, so that he has more possibilities for action in relation to a given text. This is achieved by teaching the reader to clarify his reading purpose and to continuously evaluate his experience of reading in relation to purpose. The way of reading, eye movements and processing of stimuli, is adjusted so that the greatest possible concordance is established between reading purpose and experience of content.

The methodology of reading skills training gains by concentrating on the processing of stimuli and on the experience of meaning.

WE DO OUR BEST

Or do we?

Modern man
has the skill:
he can do
what he will.
But alas –
being man
he will do
what he can.

6

Principles for
reading skills training

It is important to clarify the objectives of reading skills training. However, formulating such objectives raises a series of problems.

Objectives in Reading Skills Training

A principal difficulty with the statement of objectives is that culturally determined values will always form part of such statements. If for instance the question What is a good reader? is asked, these values immediately come

Difficulties with Statement of Objectives

into question: Is a good reader one who reads with excessive speed, or is it one who reads fiction with emphatic understanding?

Different people, and consequently different reading teachers, have their own views on what is most essential. In addition, every student has his own conception of what kind of a reader he would like to become. Therefore, an important requirement as to the formulation of objectives is that it must contain room for the student's values. A thorough exposition of various ways of describing good reading can be found in the work of Gray & Rogers (1956). It must be added, however, that the concept of "good reading" is not solely a question of cultural and personal values. It is also a product of processes and development in society: There is a strong causative relation between the rise of the technological society and the development of "speed-reading".

Another difficulty is related to the level at which one is giving the description. One may describe the objective of better reading on a personality level by means of hypothetical constructs such as attitudes, or on a behavioral level in behavioral terms. A statement of objectives on the personality level is less precise and more difficult to measure than a statement of objectives on the behavioral level. However, personality objectives include important aspects which are difficult to express in behavioral terms.

Description of Objectives on a Personality Level

A description of objectives on a personality level may comprise the entire function, "to read and to study". The training goal will in that case then be change of the students' entire reading and studying skills. The concept of skill is here understood as *whole-person-skill*.

This whole-person-skill is defined as the totality of personality factors which determine a given reading performance. Thus the objective of reading skills training becomes a change of, and consequently involves work in

84

the teaching situation with, the following parts of the readers' personality:

1. techniques such as eye movement techniques, skimming techniques, and note-taking techniques;

2. methods such as start by surveying and start by defining a reading purpose;

3. habits such as the habit of working every day, the habit of doing fast-work, always working quickly, and the habit of working in a concentrated way;

4. attitudes such as for instance an active questioning attitude or a critical attitude;

5. motivations and interests such as a wish to become knowledgeable in new areas and a wish to cope with large quantities of reading.

A description of objectives in behavioral terms may be stated generally or more specifically. In one set of materials a general wording was used: "learning to read faster and more flexibly" (Jacobsen, Jansen & Lundahl, 1972). Here the transfer to daily reading is implied in using the words "learning to read faster" instead of the words "learning to be able to read faster".

Description of Objectives on a Behavioral Level

The aim of being better at daily reading, and not just at a single reading test, may be difficult to express in more specific behavioral terms, but it is not impossible. An example of a more specific formulation, which satisfies this demand of transfer to daily work situations, is: "half a year after the termination of the course the student must be able to perform his daily reading with a reading speed, measured in w. p. m. (words per minute), which is at least 25 percent higher than before the course began; this would hold for 80 percent of publications read and for texts at the same degree of difficulty. Reading comprehension should remain at least the same."

The decision as to whether the last mentioned objective has been reached, may be based upon, 1) reading tests, 2) reports made by the student on his own reading over

Measurements of Reaching the Objective

85

one or several weeks, and 3) interviews with the student. The decision whether the condition of at least the same reading comprehension has been fulfilled, may be made on, 1) the student's self-evaluation, 2) reading tests with comprehension questions, and 3) reading followed by writing of summaries.

The Student's Own Objectives

A last, and essential, difficulty connected with the formulation of objectives is the relationship between the objectives of the course and the objectives and expectations of the student. It is decisive for the results, whether the student's objectives are inconsistent with or in accordance with the course. Therefore, it is important to give the student the possibility of choosing which parts of his reading and study skills he wants to train. The importance of the students' objectives within speed-reading training has been directly demonstrated over several years by asking students at the start of a reading course: which rate do you expect to reach?

The students' replies are as much an expression of self-evaluation as goal setting. This became apparent in one case, where a rather confident female student, who read 250 w. p. m. with easier fiction, stated with much firmness: "I want to reach 900 w. p. m." To this the teacher answered: "Well, then you will really have to do something for it." The student answered firmly: "I am going to!" She did reach her goal! This example illustrations rather well the relation between previous expectations and later results. This relation has been further clarified by a major study by Jacobsen (1971).

The Problem of Transfer

The problem of transfer is one of the most essential problems in training reading and study skills. Yet this problem is often overlooked. The problem can be stated as follows: should the students first of all aim at being able to read better on reading tests or should they primarily aim at reading better at home every day?

When a statement of objectives emphasizes that the

86

goal is daily reading, the transfer problem becomes essential: how are the newly acquired skills to be transferred from training situations to daily use?

Today many reading courses simply neglect transfer problems, which of course is the easiest answer. Usually it is assumed that if reading and study technique skills are trained and if the results are confirmed by tests, then the skills will automatically be used in the daily work. Studies such as the one mentioned by Robinson (1961), as well as daily experiences indicate that transfer to daily use is very problematic. This is especially true regarding long-term effects.

Reading Courses Which Neglect the Transfer Problem

One of the participants in a standard mechanized course in reading skills training answered a question about daily use with: "Now and then I try to use what I have learned, but as a rule I forget it and fall back." Another student told about his experience with attending study methods courses: "I learned study methods in elementary school as well as in secondary school. They told us about all the good and correct things you have to do and about all the good methods. I know it all by heart. But one never cares to use all that."

These statements exemplify in a pretty way Dewey's words: ". . . that education is not an affair of telling and being told, but an active and constructive process, a principle almost as generally violated in practice as conceded in theory" (Dewey, 1916). Within the methodology described here, it has been attempted to solve the transfer problem through an application of Dewey's learning-by-doing principle. This principle of Dewey's has had a considerable influence on Danish educational practice (Jansen, 1973).

The Learning-by-Doing Principle

What methodological consequences are to be drawn from the Dewey principle?

Possible methods

87

In many Danish reading training programs the training is built up around the pupils' daily reading. In other words, it is thought that training in better reading must take place with reading material and in work situations which are similar to the everyday reading material and the everyday work situations. Thus in speed-reading training, especially during the first weeks, fiction is used as training material. This material is very easy. The students are asked to choose some books they feel like reading and eventually books they have to read anyway. It is important that the students choose books which are easily understood and which create no problems in typography and layout. Preferably the books should be very interesting as well.

The Possible Role of Reading Machines

Transfer problems will often be accentuated by the use of reading machines, since reading with a machine is a very artificial situation compared to the average everyday reading situation. Within the methodology described here reading skills training without use of machines is consequently the most usual. The machines are seldom used as a permanent part of a program. However, due to the motivating qualities of machines, mixed solutions are occasionally used. In the following such a mixed solution is described:

Most students in the reading course receive no assistance from machines; they do well without them! During the course a few students work individually with a reading accelerator if the teacher finds that the student is getting blocked or if the teacher believes that some pressure may be useful. This may be especially true for some overcareful readers.

If a student periodically bases his work on a machine, he will eventually have to pass through a special transfer program. In that program the student starts very smoothly by letting the T-bar of the rateometer run on the opposite side of the page that is being read so that a kind

88

of indirect pacing occurs. From there the student completes a series of exercises where, for example, he reads for some minutes with the machine and then switches it off and reads for 30 minutes. The final stage is to read for 30 minutes at home without machine while trying to maintain the same speed. A description of this kind of working schedule is described by, among others, Causey & Fischer (1959).

While the use of reading machines is the exception, all students work specifically with transfer programs. In addition to answering questions each time on how they get along with newspaper reading and other daily reading, students are requested to extend the duration of their reading periods gradually.

Transfer Exercises Without Machines

A 10-minute reading test is not considered descriptive of daily reading. As soon as a student is considered ready, the teacher will suggest that the student extends his reading time so that he reaches about a 30-minute period. The final demand is to read an entire ordinary book in one evening with the newly acquired reading speed. This goal is reached by practically all students.

Students who have worked mainly with easy literature work with more difficult literature eventually. It is not taken for granted that a high reading speed acquired by reading easy literature is automatically transferred to more difficult reading material. To read difficult reading material as fast as easy material is not a realistic objective, although to read more difficult literature faster than at the start of the course is. In order to accomplish this objective, one works finally with finding one's own reading level for difficult literature.

As an example of how a complete reading skills training course may be developed so that the above-mentioned objectives and transfer problems may be solved, see Appendix D (p. 164).

Reading as a
Function of
Personality –
Not an
Isolated
Activity

In the above-mentioned description of objectives, reading skills training was viewed as an activity that concerns the entire person and her daily reading behavior.

Many reading programs seem to be based on the erroneous idea that it is possible to treat reading skills apart from the personality of the reader. But it is not possible, so to speak, to take people's eyes out of their heads, train the eye movements, and put the eyes back, and then believe that the person now reads faster than before. If somebody is afraid of not understanding everything or of missing some of the contents, it is not primarily eye movement training which is indicated. Similarly it does not help to provide training in correct note-taking techniques for students who have resentment against lectures or who do not believe in the benefit of taking notes.

Personality
as a Factor
at the Start
of the Course

When starting a reading skills training course, the personality will determine the processes and the outcome of the training. Smith (1955) has shown how personality traits were decisive in influencing the degree of progress in reading skills training. Experiences in Denmark confirm this observation and point to the significance of general capacity for work.

In this connection Danish reading course teachers have noticed a type of student that has been increasing in number during the last few years. This student makes only modest progress and seems to have difficulties in organizing his own study situation. The teachers characterize such students as follows: everything around them is a mess; they do not have much grasp of themselves; they rarely work or work diffusely, forget their notes, are late, etc.

Interactions
between
Reading and
Personality

Identical training methods are processed quite differently by different students. This is clearly apparent from conversations with the students during a reading course. Observations indicate that traits or attitudes such as:

perfectionism/conscientiousness versus sloppiness/careless-
ness, and: activity (active-aggressiveness) versus passivity
(passive-/receptiveness) influence the training process in
decisive ways. Also situationally determined short changes
of mood, energy and physical well-being strongly influence reading skills training work.

During a course daily reading performances are tre-
mendously influenced by gusto, emotional crises and
various external events. Now and then this appears with
striking clarity in the reading curves made by each student. As an example, a reading curve of one student suddenly dropped from about 700 w. p. m. to about 450.

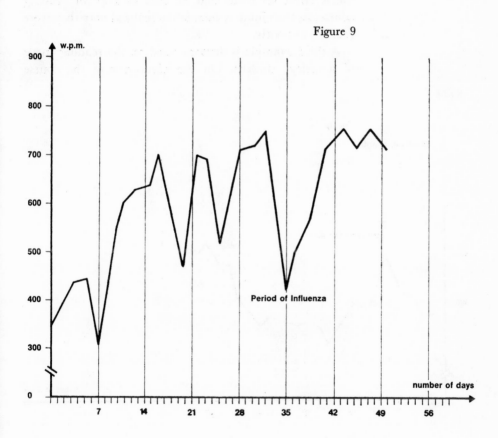

Figure 9

This decrease took place after a short period of influenza (see figure 9).

Another example comes from a class of 14- to 15-year-old pupils working with reading skills training. One of the pupils of the class died in a traffic accident on Saturday. The following Monday the other pupils in the class were shocked. Late in the morning the class started its reading skills training. The mean rate of reading for the class was below half of what was expected. The teacher felt that this documentation of how much the children were influenced by, what had happened might have so much effect on them that he had to stop the reading course, as the children themselves realized *why* they were reading so poorly.

A third example is demonstrated on the reading curve of a college student. On the ninth day of the course

Figure 10

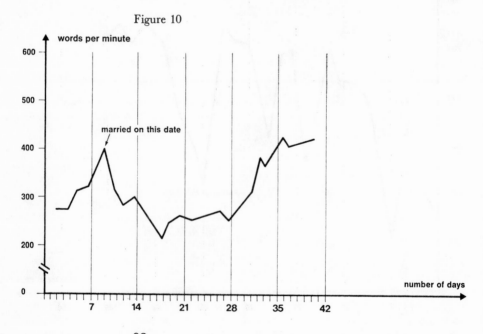

92

shown in figure 10 the student got married. It is to be seen that the time of the marriage is clearly reflected in the reading performance curve.

These examples illustrate that emotional states influence reading and study skills training. Personality states then effect reading performance. The reverse is also the case. It is usual that reading results influence emotional reactions quite markedly. With demonstrated competence and progress students express pleasure and pride. They feel good. In contrast, plateaus on the reading curve are often accompanied by sullenness and disappointment. This disappointment over lack of progress may in turn influence the amount of energy put into training, so that a vicious circle may commence and continue for a time.

Reading Performances also Influence the Emotions

All such ramifications, all these interactions between reading and personality, are very complicated. The important task for the reading course teacher is to try to take all these aspects into account. The difficult task is to integrate this knowledge into one's educational thinking and practice.

THOSE WHO KNOW

Those who always
know what's best
are
a universal pest.

7.

Reading skills training for adults.

Description of an individualized method

Experiences with individualized reading skills training that apply the educational principles discussed in the previous chapter will be described. The majority of these experiences has been obtained from the individual lesson where one teacher instructs one student. These methods have also been adapted to group instruction, still with an emphasis on individualization of teaching. This chapter then is *an outline of a systematic method for individualized reading skills training for adults.*

94

A reading skills training course with individual lessons usually consists of nine weeks' instruction. The student receives about one quarter of an hour's instruction per week. In addition he trains by himself two or three hours per week. The course is voluntary. When the students attend the first lesson, they have been through some compulsory introductory lessons (cf. p. 68). Therefore the students arrive with some knowledge of the psychology of reading and of their own reading level through reading tests.

This form of instruction is not very expensive since an average of nine quarter hours per student is not much more time than that used by courses in small groups. However, individual instruction is nearly always experienced as effective and satisfactory by teacher and student. A fairly comparable kind of instruction is used in special education of young people and adults who are retarded in reading. Here individual teaching is practically just as economical as group instruction. Furthermore it is decidedly effective.

The course may be divided into sequences. The description which follows has been developed from a student with speed training and skimming as goals for her instruction. In principle the instruction would not be fundamentally different if other goals had been established, for instance study skills training.

The main content of the first lesson is the diagnostic interview. The teacher attempts to get a general view of the student's reading and study situation. The student's reading level, way of reading and reading habits are mapped out. Then a provisional schedule is made comprising tentative decisions as to the objectives and content of the training. When this schedule is agreed upon, the teacher gives training directions for the following week.

The teacher makes a few notes about each single

The Framework of Individual Reading Skills Training

The Structure of the Instructional Sequences

The First Lesson

95

student. This note-making is continued throughout the course. The teacher usually does not fill in a standardized form but takes notes based upon his immediate experience of the situation.

The Following Week

During the following week the student trains at home for about four periods of 30–45 minutes each. This is done in books chosen by the student. He makes a weekly report on his work and starts a reading curve (see p. 101ff.). The weekly report and the reading curve are used as the student's own work journal.

The Second Lesson

In the second lesson the teacher and student evaluate the work of the first week from the report and the reading curve. The student also provides an account of difficulties experienced during the work. The teacher gives new training directions based upon the apparent difficulties.

Lessons Three through Nine

Lessons three–nine are in their structure similar to lesson two. Homework and lessons alternate until the teacher and students agree on terminating the course. This usually takes place after about nine weeks. There may now and then be shorter or longer courses according to individual needs.

Three Levels of Work

The course of activities is outlined in figure 11.

In the diagram three groups of activities in the course are shown. At the bottom is training work where the student trains by reading in a book. In the middle are those activities where the student evaluates his training by counting words, calculating rate, making the weekly report and the reading curve. At the top the instruction in individual lessons is described which consists of evaluation of the work together with the teacher and of agreeing upon directions on the work to follow.

96

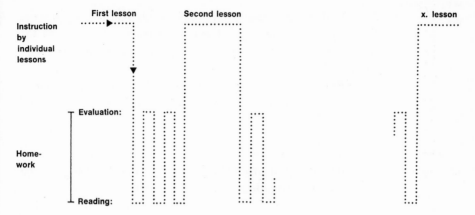

Figure 11

This provides only a summary of the types of activities. A more complete description is presented below.

The diagnostic interview includes a variety of topics. The student's wishes regarding the objectives and content of the instruction are examined. The student discusses her reading and studying problems. The student's test results are discussed, but the teacher makes no effort to have the objectives and content of instruction decided solely on the basis of these results. A provisional schedule of instruction is developed and outlined in writing.

If the student decides on speed training as a training objective, she is asked what rate is being aimed at. This goal is noted. Whenever the student primarily wants speed training, the teacher tries to get an impression of reading problems such as regressions, inner voice and overconscientious reading.

What may be of particular importance is to summarize the student's previous history in reading and studying work. This would include reading difficulties at school, attitudes towards reading and learning, amount of children's literature read and the development of these aspects through various classes.

If the objective is training in study reading, the teacher tries to locate where the difficulties lie according to the student's own experience. Teacher and student together consider aspects such as study motivation, work habits, work methods, attitudes towards and interest in particular subjects as well as relations to fellow students and teachers.

Training in books

Training in books takes place at home and is the essential part of the instruction. Students primarily train on their own daily reading and study material, i. e. books they have to read anyway or would like to read. Often this training is based upon specific instructions.

As a rule, speed training starts on easier fiction. This practice is based on the point of view that training of skills goes more smoothly when one problem is taken up at a time. Easy fiction does not present problems of understanding and of speed technique at the same time.

One attempts to work primarily with the student's own daily material in order to increase motivation. The student should not set aside a great deal of extra time for special reading skills training since if he uses daily material there will be double benefit from the work. Furthermore there will not be the same problems of transfer as when working with special training material.

If the student has a very modest reading speed, or if persistent lack of progress occurs during book training, it may be advisable for a period of time to simplify greatly the comprehensibility of the reading material with which the student works.

Forms of Reading Training

A summary of forms of training which are frequently used is presented. This list may at first appear surprisingly simple. The simplicity is intended: it is in accordance with the view that becoming a better reader is not a technical, sophisticated matter, it is a simple personal matter. The training forms presented here, together with

98

the weekly report, the reading curve, and the instructional discussions (described later), constitute the core of the method. When reading the following it is to be remembered that individual adjustments are always made.

One form of training involves reading for 10–15 minutes and then calculating the rate in words per minute. The main aim of this practice is not testing but training. The student is instructed to do this practice in a book of own choice, for instance four times during the first week.

1.
Read and
Calculate
the Rate

A second form is similar to the first except that a speed card is used. A speed card is a white or grey card, 15×20 centimeters, which is moved down across the page so that it covers the lines just read. The speed card has proved very useful in eliminating regressions and in pressing for higher speed. A speed card is the opposite of a card used by beginners as a help not to skip the line. (This latter card is placed below the line and has a different function.)

2.
Use of
Speed Card

A third form consists of periods of ordinary reading alternating with periods of spurt reading. In spurt reading the rate is deliberately increased 50–110 percent without consideration for understanding. (Actually, spurt reading is identical with some type of skimming.)

3.
Spurt
Reading

This kind of training is generally experienced as very effective. It is similar to paperback scanning developed at the University of Michigan in the United States. This has also proven very effective, in fact more effective than various forms of machine training (Braam & Berger, 1968).

In the beginning, when spurt reading is used, the training is arranged in three parts: A) a period of ordinary reading (for instance warming up for two minutes), B) a period of ordinary reading calculating the rate (such as 10 minutes) and C) a period of spurt reading for perhaps three minutes. The form is called *A-B-C training*. Spurt reading is placed last because an adaptation to this form of training is necessary. It is experienced as rather demanding at the start. General comments from students confirm this: "my eyes swim"; "I can make nothing of it"; "you cannot read that way"; "it is tough on the book".

When adaptation to spurt reading has taken place, it is placed in the middle of three five-minute training periods. This form is called *5-5-5 training*. The intermediate period of spurt reading will often have a positive effect on the rate of ordinary reading during the last five minutes! Student reactions to this form are generally very favorable.

4
Extension of Reading Time

A fourth form of training involves extension of reading time (= transfer exercises). The length of the reading periods is systematically extended with the aim of transfer to daily reading.

5.
Reading for Plot

A fifth form of training is reading for the main plot. Here one works not with easy children's books as previously described but with books which are not specially interesting or important to the reader. One consciously works towards the aim of reading solely for experiencing the plot and ignoring the details.

6.
Establishing and Reaching a Goal

A sixth form of training involves establishing and reaching a goal within a certain time period. The student, or sometimes the student and the teacher, set up a goal of how many pages he should read in a book within, for instance, half an hour. The student places a slip of paper at the place in the book which he should reach. The slip must be easily seen. Then the student places his watch before him and starts to read.

100

Besides these forms of training in books, exercises on special material are occasionally used. There may be single technical exercises in perceptual training. Striking out exercises may also be used, i.e. striking out all less essential words in a text. For this purpose it is not necessary to use special material. Newspapers and paperbacks are excellent materials.

7.
*Other
Forms of
Reading
Training*

The students write reports and draw reading curves in relation to their work at home. Each time the student has trained in a book, she calculates the rate and makes a self-evaluation of understanding. For this self-evaluation she may use word descriptions or a scale. Some students use a "3 + 1 scale". The three points consist of above average, average and below average. The +1 is used to indicate understanding that is outside judgment for some reason. This "3 + 1" scale has proved very useful in much educational evaluation, as "+1" functions like an anchor counteracting a tendency for evaluation to slide upwards, or downwards if it comes to that. "+1" represents the decidedly unusual.

*Weekly Report
and Reading
Curve*

At the beginning some students may resist having to evaluate their own understanding. When this is particularly persistent they may use reading tests with comprehension questions. However, they should be urged to change to self-evalutation and, in cases of doubt, to base their evaluation on written summaries. A teacher argument which is difficult for the student to reject is, "after the course is finished, just one person will be able to evaluate whether there has been satisfactory benefit in your reading – yourself!"

The weekly report records the time, nature and amount of work done. It provides information on reading speed (rate – words per minute) and comprehension. Special circumstances can also be noted such as fatique, difficulties or illness. The student records reflections on his own

Weekly Reports

101

Name: Tom Jones

date	hour	title	number of pages read	duration (minutes)	comprehension	rate (w.p.m.)
Nov. 3rd	3rd lesson	"Silver Chief"	21	20	good	290
Nov. 3rd	9¹⁵ p.m.	"Silver Chief"	18	20	OK, but sleepy	261
Nov. 6th.	about 4 p.m.	"Silver Chief" Last part	26	25	quite good	291
Nov. 8th	1-2 p.m.	"Black Horse"	34	20	speed training	413

1. I succeeded in:

Comprehension is quite OK, but I seem to be stuck about 280 w.p.m.

2. I did not succeed in:

It is a bit hard to read at home the number of times we planned

3. Next week I intend to

continue speed reading, and maybe find a new book for ordinary reading

Figure 12

reading skills training: success, lack of success and intentions for the next week.

Two illustrations of weekly reports are indicated in figures 12 and 13. As can be seen they are quite individualistic, representing the characteristics of each student.

102

Weekly report No.: _____

Name: _Barbara Smith_

date	hour	title	number of pages read	duration (minutes)	comprehension	rate (w.p.m.)
Oct. 20th	8:00 – 9:00 a.m.	"Tortilla Flat"	26	15	not too good (C)	610
Oct. 21th	8:00 – 9:00 a.m.	"Tortilla Flat"	24	15	fine! (a)	540
Oct. 23th	12:00 – 1:00 p.m.	"The Sailors"	16	15	medium (B)	450
Oct. 24th	Home in the evening	"The Sailors"	32	27	fine (a)	560

1. I succeeded in:

The two first times and the last one. The inner voice has disappeared most of the time.

2. I did not succeed in:

To start on a new book – I find that difficult

3. Next week I intend to

reach a rate of 600 w. p. m. on "The Sailors."

Figure 13

At the start of the course the teacher makes clear that the only indispensable demand in the instruction is that the student must deliver a report every week no matter what the volume and quality of his work are. Experience shows that the weekly report will quickly have a support-

ive effect on the work of the student. At the beginning
the report-making may be stressful for students who hold
distorted self-images regarding their own working capacity.

Reading Curves

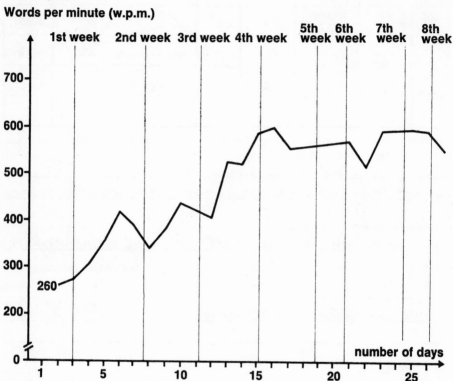

Figure 14
This is a typical reading curve. The student's perception of the
problems and the training directions given by the teacher are
shown in the following 3 parts of the curve.

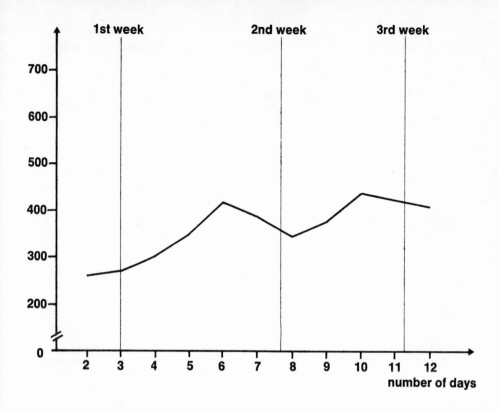

	1st week	2nd week	3rd week	
Reading problems as perceived by the student	Regressions. My eyes jump down before line is finished and have to go up again. (Was confirmed by teacher observing the student's eye movements)	"Change of line" exercises worked out well. Worked with speed card below the line. The clock irritates me. My thoughts are running during the reading. Feel the inner voice.	Regressions probably disappeared. Inner voice very disturbing.	
Training directions given by the teacher	1. Read 10 minutes in book; then "change of line" exercises. (1+2 3 + 4) Then read 10 minutes again. 2. Use the speed card. 3. Use the special "window card", i.e. a card with an oval hole for words.	1. Read 30 minutes alternately with and without speed card. 2. Eventually use "change of line" exercises just before reading.	ABC-exercises	

Figure 14. Part one

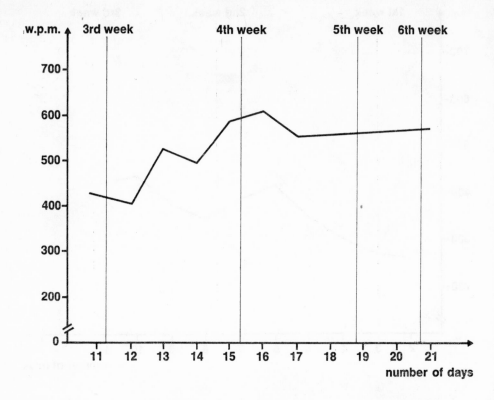

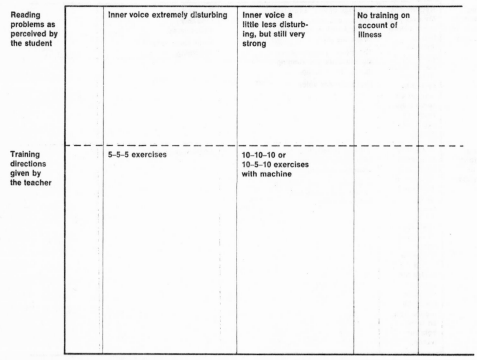

Figure 14. Part two

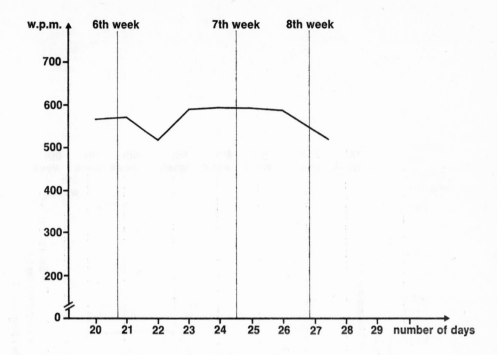

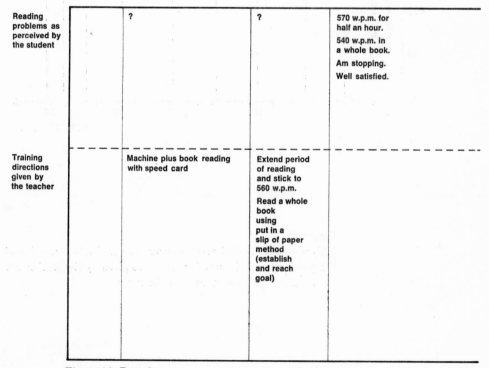

Figure 14. Part three

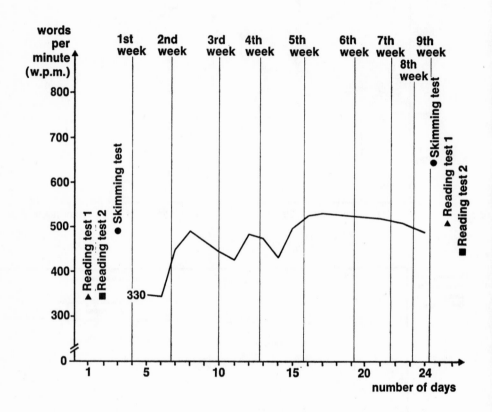

Figure 15
This is another typical reading curve. The student's perception of
the problems and the training directions given by the teacher are
shown in the following 3 parts of the curve.

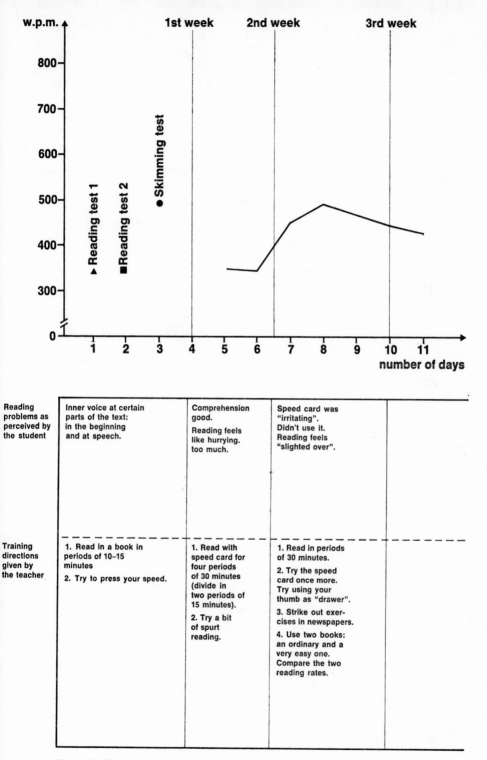

Figur 15. Part one

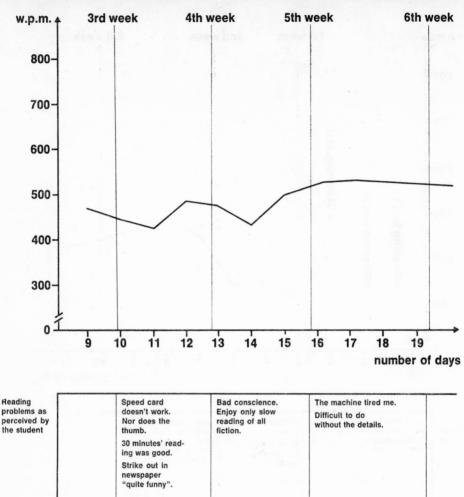

| w.p.m. | 3rd week | 4th week | 5th week | 6th week |

number of days

Reading problems as perceived by the student	Speed card doesn't work. Nor does the thumb. 30 minutes' reading was good. Strike out in newspaper "quite funny".	Bad conscience. Enjoy only slow reading of all fiction.	The machine tired me. Difficult to do without the details.	
Training directions given by the teacher	1. Try reading machine if speed card "doesn't work". 2. Extend reading from 30 to 45 minutes. 3. Try more strike out in newspaper exercises. 4. Train in an easy book.	1. Train deliberately non-careful reading. 2. Read non-involving literature with machine. 3. Read for the main plot.	1. Use the machine for two days. a. 30 minutes of transfer exercise b. 5 minutes with machine, 20 minutes without, 5 minutes with machine. 2. Read at home for 30 minutes the next two days.	

Figur 15. Part two

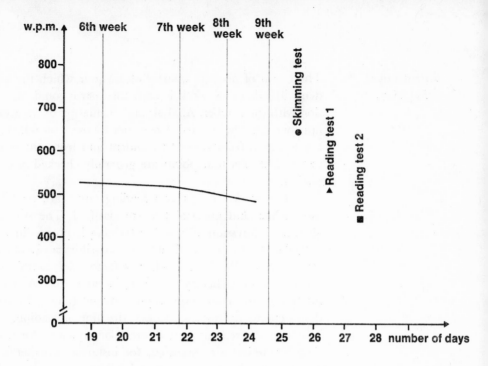

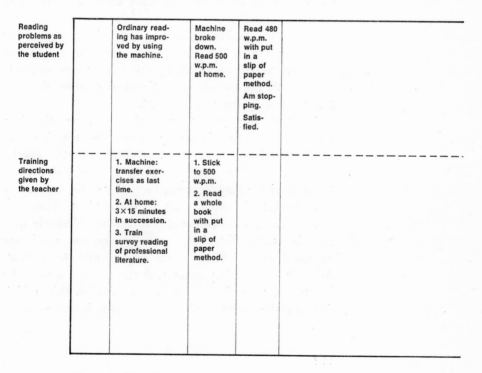

Figure 15. Part three

Instructional Discussions

The lesson of about a quarter of an hour which the student attends every week is used for instructional discussion with the teacher. Analysis and evaluation of the work are covered. The discussion does not follow a set schedule but is varied from student to student and from one week to the next. Yet four points are generally checked in succession.

1. The weekly report and reading curve are read by the teacher and uncertainties are clarified. The student gives his impression of how the training is proceeding.

2. Based on report and curve the possible causes of the results are explored. A number of factors are examined: the degree of difficulty of a certain book, the student's interest in the book, typography and language, the student's energy during the reading, the time of reading, the length of the reading period, etc. Consequences for continued training are discussed, for instance, whether another book should be used or other training hours might be better.

3. Reading problems that occur are discussed, i. e. the difficulties which the student experiences in connection with her reading work. All aspects of what goes on inside and outside the person are explored as possible obstacles for progress in the reading work.

4. Finally the teacher gives training advice, directions for the next week. They may concern the length of the reading periods, the kind of reading material, special forms of training, etc. According to the student, the training advice may be in the form of general suggestions with further elaboration left to the student. They can also be given as more detailed directions. Similarly they may be stated directively or as suggestions which are discussed and modified by the teacher and the student. Again it is most important that the teacher adapts the instruction to each student. To accomplish this a high degree of flexibility on the teacher's part is necessary.

Every process of work has a cognitive as well as an affective side. Authors like John Dewey (1910) and N. R. F. Maier (1963) in different epochs described the affective side, the emotional processes of work.

In reading skills training various emotional reactions are usual. These may be rather intense, especially at reading curve plateaus, or when the student is confronted with imperfections in his work habits. It is usual for people who attend reading skills training now and then to experience quite strong emotional reactions. These feelings vary from being irritated and disappointed to being happy and proud.

One type of emotional reaction deserves special attention. It has been called "dullness of training". Individual students on certain days seem remarkably dull, that is they seemingly display a very low energy, a low interest in training and appear somewhat pessimistic in their attitude. (In group instruction this phenomenon may even occur as a sort of "group emotion" of sullenness and irritation.) What does the teacher do when such feelings occur? It is important to mention these phenomena at the start of the course. The teacher's task is also to have the student experience and express the feelings which training has brought about.

When emotional pressure is decreased, there will be more energy left for the intellectual process. To accomplish this purpose the teacher should master certain attitudes and techniques. He should be attentive to latent, easily overlooked feelings which lie below manifest factual verbalizations. The teacher should refrain from interfering during pauses while the student is thinking and from arguing or evaluating the student's emotions as they are being expressed. He may encourage the student to expand on the difficulties or ask for specific examples. Also the teacher might use Rogers' "reflection of feelings" by reformulating the student's way of thinking and at-

113

tempting to clarify its emotional content. Reassurance can be given by telling that others have also felt the same way.

Intellectual
Facilitation
When emotional aspects of the reading problems are clarified, there is a better possibility for processing thoughts. In Dewey's words, "the emotionally accentuated problem is intellectually transformed into a problem to be solved – into a question, which demands an answer" ... "A condition for this transformation is a closer observation of the facts, which form the problem, and which are the cause of the fact that action is impeded." In order to facilitate intellectual transformation to the acknowledgement of problems, the teacher will generally ask the student some questions. These questions concretize and specify the student's experience of and observations on his own reading. The questions search for the obstacles or difficulties in relation to the objective: to read faster. These obstacles, such as the inner voice, must be identified and defined.

Now and then, especially at the start of training, the teacher may ask the student to read a text on the spot. During the reading the teacher can observe eye movements directly. Immediately after he can ask questions about the student's experience of his way of reading.

From the instructional discussion one or two reading problems can be identified as obstacles to continued progress. It is on these facts the teacher builds his suggestions for training the next week. In a summary of methods for research on the reading process Strang wrote, "much can be learned about the reading process through students' retrospective and introspective verbalization" (Strang, 1968). The teaching described here is aimed at integrating this point of view into everyday teaching.

From Reading
Diagnosis to ...
The teacher makes diagnostic considerations throughout the course. This may sound very complicated, but ac-

114

tually it simply refers to the teacher's reflections on and analyses of the characteristic reading and study behaviors of each student at various times. Instructional discussion provides the material for these considerations. Sometimes the teacher writes down small diagnostic notes comprising impressions, descriptions and reading rates. Some of these diagnostic thoughts are discussed with the students; others are not.

The diagnostic considerations form the basis of developing the weekly training program. The word "program" should be understood in its broadest meaning. For instance, the teacher's behavior may be included as an element consciously varied according to the diagnosis. The teacher will be more nondirective and more accepting towards some students than to others.

The chart below provides some guidelines for the choice of training directions in relation to certain diagnosed difficulties:

Diagnosis		*Specified Training*
1. Regressions	→	1. training with speed card
2. Inner voice	→	2. spurt reading
3. Overconscientious reading	→	3. instructional discussion and training in loose reading
4. Difficulties with transfer	→	4. transfer exercises (for instance extension of reading time)
5.a Passive, uncertain and anxious student behavior	→	5.a highly structured training directions
5.b Autonomous, purposeful, active student behavior	→	5.b training directions with low structure
6.a Weak motivation	→	6.a much support from teacher, work with emotional reactions
6.b Strong motivation	→	6.a little support, the teacher sets challenges, work with intellectual facilitation

115

Reading skills
Training
Through Group
Instruction

Group instruction has been used for different groups such as university students, teachers, engineers and mixed groups of adults from different professions.

Important
Prerequisites

University students usually start with some previous instructional lessons. From these they have some knowledge of study and work habits and of the psychology of reading. They have some information about their own reading ability based on tests. When participants do not start with this background, it is included in the instruction as problem-solving discussions in small groups. These matters are dealt with during the two first lessons. They have an important function in motivating the participants, assisting in the development of a positive climate of work in the group, and establishing appropriate working norms in the group.

The Procedure
of Instruction

The procedure of instruction parallels the activities in individual training described on p. 95ff. Only deviations from those activities will be described.

The First
Lesson

In the first lesson the participants in turn express their wishes regarding the objectives and content of the instruction. These wishes are written down and the teacher sketches a rough outline of a plan which, as far as possible, meets and coordinates the expressed wishes. This outline is discussed, changed and finally decided upon by the group. The participants' test results are noted by the teacher.

Then the participants individually describe their reading habits and other reading and work problems. In some groups an exchange of experiences between participants starts at this time. The teacher writes down key information, which he will use later in formulating training advice. Finally, training advice is given for the next

116

week. As a rule it is better to formulate these directions rather precisely.

The second lesson evaluates the work and difficulties of the first week, as previously described (cf. p. 96).

The subsequent lessons will vary in content. But as a rule, certain activities will be repeated each time. These activities are:

The Following Lessons

A short exposition of a topic from the psychology of reading or studying will be presented by one or two participants from an assigned article or manual.

1.
Exposition
of a Topic

The participants train for about 10–15 minutes in books of their own choice that they have brought to the lessons. This may be used to confirm the speeds which the participants have stated that they have obtained in training at home. New forms of training may also be introduced and practiced for instance 5-5-5 training (cf. p. 100). At the same time the teacher has some minutes to read the weekly reports and make feedback notes. It is very useful if this can be done during the lesson, as it permits an immediate individual feedback.

2.
Training
during Lessons

While the participants calculate their reading speed, the teacher talks for a short time with each individual. The information obtained this way may be used in future work.

3.
Calculating
Reading Speed

Group discussion corresponds to the individual instructional discussion described on p. 112. Sometimes it may be supplemented with informal individual discussion during a pause or before or after the lesson.

4.
Group
Instructional
Discussion

The teacher gives training directions for the next week either individually or to the group.

5.
Training
Directions

117

Group discussion is a difficult form of teaching to many teachers. There are differences in this form from one teacher to the other. Generally the discussion may be focused successfully on an analysis of the reasons for the results and on the reading problems of each participant. In the analysis of the reason for the results the teacher often takes the initiative by asking individual participants questions. A discussion of reading problems may start a profitable exchange of experience in the group. For instance, one participant may feel disturbed by a strong inner voice and cannot understand how it is possible to read without this inner voice. Another may report that she has had the same difficulty, but now has broken through by means of a certain activity.

In discussions of reading problems the teacher attempts to progress from a teacher-centered process to a teacher-facilitated group interaction, as indicated by the diagrams in figure 16.

The rationale corresponds to that expressed for reme-dial teaching: ". . . an effective group is not formed by simply collecting a group of retarded readers, for, without cohesion, leadership and esprit reading progress is weak" (Spache, 1963). The group discussion described here is not a collection of individuals each of whom discuss their reading problems with the teacher. A teacher-facilitated group discussion may be fostered by a range of techniques on the part of the teacher, such as: dividing the group into groups of four during the first lessons, preparing questions for discussion between the participants, allowing the content of instruction to be directed by group decisions, asking the group members in turn to make three- or four-minute summaries of articles or chapters in books, arranging for sharing emotions and attitudes towards work habits, work inhibitions and motivation, and finally letting the group evaluate its own way of working.

Figure 16

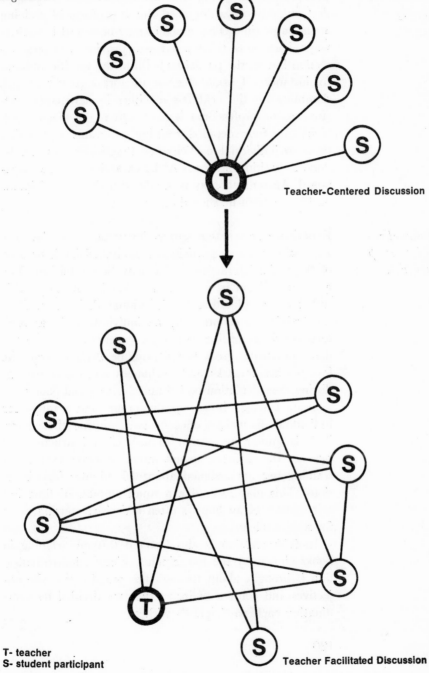

Teacher-Centered Discussion

T- teacher
S- student participant

Teacher Facilitated Discussion

Directions for Training

The problem in giving training directions for a group is that everyone does not need the same form of training at the same time. This problem may be solved in various ways. Sometimes the teacher will provide a general direction but let the participants fill in the specific content, for instance: "I would like you to work a great deal with skimming for the next lesson, either in newspapers, periodicals or professional books." Often the teacher will give three-four detailed training programs and assign these to individual participants. Practically this can be done by writing program A, B, C, and D on the blackboard. Agreements may be made with single participants on the program he should select.

Individualization in Group Instruction

Experience shows that group instruction may be very successful for those participants motivated for it because of the social interaction which may be established. The greatest problem in group instruction is how to provide sufficient consideration for individual differences. How the training directions may be individualized has been mentioned. According to teacher experiences and to student statements great benefit can be derived from the few teacher remarks and exchanges with each student during the calculation period and during small pauses.

Some teachers break up the group and arrange for individual discussions once or twice during the course. This is similar in pattern to individual instruction. In practice the students do not attend a whole evening of training but are assigned about 15 minutes for discussions. This may seem like a small amount of time but this quarter of an hour is often a decisive starting point for some students.

Individualization is also fostered through training in books chosen by the participants. Finally, individualization is brought about through the practice that the objectives and content of instruction are decided by coordinating each participant's wishes.

120

LAST THINGS FIRST

Solutions to problems
  are easy to find:
the problem's a great
  contribution.
What is truly an art
  is to wring from your mind
a problem to fit
  a solution.

8.

Reading problems as described by students

A survey was made of commonly occurring reading problems as perceived by students. By reading problems is here understood the unsatisfactory aspects of one's reading; that is, the perceived difficulties (blockings, hindrances) in relation to one's reading or reading progress.

The survey consisted of collecting material from 150 college students and adults who participated in reading skills training courses. The material included the weekly written reports of the participants, and the teacher's notations of typical remarks occurring during the reading skills training lessons. All these statements were then

The Character of the Survey

divided into five categories according to assumed causative factors and their consequences in relation to the
training. When student remarks were interpreted according to the scheme, this often seemed to result in
progress of the work.

*Application of
the Survey to
Diagnosis and
Training*

It is important for a teacher to be able to diagnose reading and study problems with reasonable certainty.

It is no less important to be able to formulate training
directions with a high degree of probability of their being
successful. The experiences and considerations developed
from this survey may be used by the teacher for diagnostic considerations and formulations of training directions. However, it should be emphasized that what is presented here is not a thoroughly validated diagnostic category system; rather it is a series of examples from which
each teacher in various teaching situations may derive
some benefit.

What follows are some typical illustrations of each of
the five categories of reading problems, then an interpre-
tation of possible causes, and finally, consequences regarding training advice are offered.

*1.
Technical
Problems in
Reading*

*- Illustrations
of Problems*

"I often look back in the text."

"I have concurrent lip movements with professional
literature."

"My eyes won't move fast enough."

"My eyes move in jumps, at first a little too far down
and then up again."

"I have an inner voice which shouts."

"My inner voice is sometimes gone, but returns regularly."

"It seems to me that the understanding gets worse
whenever I spurt."

"The rate is impeded by the many new names in the
book."

122

This group of problems reflects phenomena which are often described in reading technique training books as concurrent speech movements, regressions and inner voice. These statements can be explained rather satisfactorily through the traditional knowledge of the psychology of reading. They are called reading technique problems. The most common problems are regressions and inner voice. Each of these are found in 50–80 percent of the participants of reading skills training courses.

– Possible Causes

As a rule regressions are effectively corrected through the use of a speed card and usually they are easily overcome. In comparison it will often demand weeks of work to get rid of the inner voice. Adults having a constant and complete inner voice will often show a plateau on the reading curve at about 325 w. p. m. However, a person with an inner voice experienced as fragmentary in certain cases may achieve a reading performance of 550–650 w. p. m. The inner voice is corrected by exercises in changing between ordinary reading and spurt reading, for instance A-B-C-training and 5-5-5-training (cf. p. 99–100).

– Training Recommendations

"Whenever I think of the eye movements, the reading speed gets worse, and I do not understand, what I have read."
"I cannot read with a watch in front of me."
"It is unpleasant to feel pressed."
"The speed card is no good; the reading gets worse."
"The machine disturbs more than it helps."
"I feel dizzy/get tired in my eyes/get a headache."
"I can spurt for two minutes only, then everything floats."

2. Adaptation to New Forms of Reading

– Illustrations of Problems

Problems of this sort often occur during the first two or three weeks of a reading skills training course. They may be explained as temporary inconveniences and irritation

– Possible Causes

created by the adaption to the reading skills training itself and to the new forms of training. Such annoyances will often occur whenever habits and attitudes are to be changed (cf. for instance, habits of smoking or eating). An important fact about these problems is that they are temporary.

The temporary feelings of irritation occur so frequently that certain teachers, especially group teachers, simply consider the so-called "dullness of training" as a phenomenon that takes place quite regularly about the third lesson after two or three weeks of training (cf. p. 113).

– Training Recommendations

The teacher may point out from the start that these phenomena usually occur. It may be an advantage to prepare the students to expect them. When the irritations start, the teacher might reassure the participants by saying that others have had the same experience and then change the directions for training slightly, but mainly proceed along the same track.

3.
Attitudes toward Reading

– Illustrations of Problems

"The enjoyment is spoiled."

"I cannot see why it is necessary to read so fast; in fact I would rather feel good."

"I'm sorry for the author when I read so fast because he has made such great efforts."

"I feel worried that my understanding is not good enough."

"In my opinion one should know all of it."

"I'm afraid to loose the details; scamping is wrong."

"I cannot decide which kind of literature really can be read quickly."

"I'm able to at the course (at school) but not at home. When I'm at home, I want to feel comfortable."

"When I read, I sort of keep in the back of my head that I have to retell it afterwards."

– Possible Causes

This group of problems borders on the previous one. Certain forms of reading can be practiced only to a

124

limited extent because of certain attitudes in the reader. A frequently occurring problem is the overconscientious reader. The reader expresses her need to have to read all details thoroughly in order to feel comfortable. Occasionally, overconscientious reading may be disguised as a case of persistent regressions or inner voice. Then the corresponding training advice will have no effect.

A good place to begin is where the reader can recognize that he has a certain way of reading which directly impedes other necessary forms of reading. To such a reader the teacher will often say that it is not a question of having one and only one form of reading. The detailed reading for enjoyment where one reads everything is also necessary and should not be destroyed. But one must command several forms and be able to vary one's reading. The teacher may recommend that the student read children's books, magazines or other kinds of reading material without too much involvement beside his ordinary reading material.

– Training Recommendations

He may also ask the student to define his purpose in reading a certain book, and then make the student stick to this purpose.

A third method involves working with newspaper articles where the student crosses out all the small words which are not necessary to get the meaning. This may convince the student that there is something that can be omitted. Finally the student may read two chapters, one as he generally does and the other without consideration for the content. Afterwards summaries are made of both chapters. Comparing the two summaries, one will often be able to demonstrate that they are equally good.

"The speed is slowed down as soon as I don't use the speed card."

"Tiredness after five minutes (lower rate)."

"I fall back when I don't read with the watch in front of me."

4.
Automation,
Transfer and
Application of
New Reading
Skills

125

– Illustrations of Problems	"I read a whole book last night. My rate fell from 750 to 475. Is this course any good at all?"
– Possible Causes	These problems are associated with attempts to automate the new reading skills so that they can be used daily and can last for the future. Students are often attentive to the problem of whether a newly acquired reading speed will hold. This transfer problem is described more thoroughly on p. 86ff.
– Training Recommendations	Transfer problems may be taken up partly in conversations about how daily reading is proceeding, such as reading without timing, newspaper reading, and professional reading. They may also be remedied systematically by specially designed transfer exercises.
5. Work Habits and Work Planning *– Illustrations of Problems*	"My reading results are immensely varied." "I cannot concentrate on boring professional literature." "Other thoughts occur constantly; I sort of run two courses of thought all the time." "I don't get anything done." "I don't get the time for it." "I am much too tired in the evening." "I am interrupted all the time."
– Possible Causes	This group of reading problems is related to the ability to concentrate, the planning of work, and the general attitude and motivation towards work. These problems nearly always have a personal side. Seen as personal problems, they usually lie outside the reading teacher's field of work and competence (IRA, 1969).
– Training Recommendations	However, the same problems may also be viewed and approached from technical and methodical aspects. The reading teacher may in this sense deal with problems of this type.

126

Regarding habits of work there may be various ways of work planning. The teacher may suggest various methods of planning. He may also suggest an analysis of the daily work conditions and work routines of the student. A discussion of inhibiting and facilitating factors may be helpful.

Difficulties in concentration with professional literature are sometimes remedied if the student learns more active methods of study reading. Although concentration problems may have many roots, it is now and then amazing to see the results which can be obtained by a thorough instruction in active, structuring methods of handling a textbook.

Man's a kind
of Missing Link
fondly thinking
he can think.

9.

Now what?
- some further questions

This book began with a series of questions which pointed to a different, more varied view on reading and reading processes. The content of the book presents a broad approach to reading, hence the title, "The Teaching of Reading–without Really Any Method". Not only have thoughts and suggestions for reading programs been described, but the book also deals with ideas, which more or less have been realized.

But what are the future unsolved problems in the psychology of reading and the methodology of teaching reading? Here, three problems will be outlined. Decisive solutions are definitely not claimed but possible ones are stated.

Language is a means of communication. Spoken and written languages are codes enabling human beings to establish contact with each other. An essential problem to a new member of a society is the mastering of this code – understanding the language. This is clearly seen with children, and it is also seen with immigrants.

Watching an adult immigrant one will notice that this development forms gradually. The immigrant will hear uniform sentences, modulations, and words repeated many times in different contexts. Gradually meaning develops. In fact it is impossible to tell whether an immigrant knows a concept or not. There are smooth transitions. Concepts gradually obtain more volume and content and the language becomes more differentiated.

Meaning does not lie in the words but is put into the words by the person who speaks or reads. This parallels the development of the child's language. The child's learning of language, listening, speaking, reading and writing, is slowly developed. It is driven by a need to understand and to communicate with the surrounding environment.

The child takes his first steps into the world of reading long before going to school. The child reads when he recognizes gas stations or candy shops by the flags and symbols of these places. The child also reads when he recognizes cornflakes and oatmeal by the package symbols. Reading is an understanding of symbolic representation. The thoughts emerging from a 4-year-old child when seeing these symbols correspond with the comprehension of the adult when reading. Thus reading from the very first steps is a process of thoughts initiated by visual symbols.

Experience also shows that, especially in elementary reading instruction, fundamental and elementary abilities are necessary in reading. For most pupils they are abilities which are most effectively trained by a very systematic

Reading is Thinking

– As Well as Mechanics

129

learning situation. Experience shows that if the child is not highly developed linguistically, free and unsystematic basic instruction will be detrimental to the learning of reading.

The argument against this viewpoint is based on highly intelligent children often from highly stimulating linguistic environments and on teachers who cannot manage systematic instruction. Therefore it is a task for the future to find a balance between the two points of view described. It is an essential educational task for the teaching of reading.

WHO IS LEARNED?

A definition

One who, consuming midnight oil
in studies diligent and slow,
teaches himself, with painful toil,
the things that other people know.

Question 1

It is possible to integrate reading as thinking and reading as mechanics in a theory of reading? If so, how is such a theory utilized in the teaching itself?

It is disadvantageous if the learning of the mother tongue language mainly consists of learning of words detached from context and meaning. In that case too much importance is placed on the symbols themselves and not on the content and meaning of the symbols. Reading is removed from the child's world of experience. Reading becomes an artificial activity which at most may have significance in single reading lessons.

In practice such purely mechanical learning is not used in Denmark today. Textbooks which contain purely mechanical learning of disconnected letters, syllables, and words are not discussed. They are passé. However, there is discussion of other parts of the content in educational materials.

Content of Textbooks Detached from the World of Experience

It should be emphasized that, if the meaning of words is not emphasized right from the first reading instruction, it may be difficult to have pupils experience reading as a process of thoughts later on. To incorporate effective thinking in reading ability, instruction must be planned in a way which immediately relates the daily experience of the child to the content of the educational materials and to the situations of instruction. Therefore, instruction should be based on the child's own pattern of language. The content of the educational material must correspond with the daily world of experience of the pupils.

The World of Experience the Child Already Has

In opposition to this, is another point of view. It is the task of the school to enlarge the pupil's world of experience. If the pupils have a relatively narrow background of experience, it is the task of the school to enlarge this background by providing information on other environments and other situations. In many places this has raised a demand that quite elementary educational materials include descriptions of environments which are unknown to the pupils but do not need to be unknown. If this ideal demand changes children's textbooks to a

– Or the World of Experience the Child Ought to Have

131

large extent, it is inevitable that this will conflict with the idea that content should reflect the experience which the child already has.

STRIKING A BALANCE

Mere good intentions go for naught.
The balance we must strike
consists of liking what we ought
and doing what we like.

Question 2

Is it possible that the content of elementary textbooks balance the demands for the pupil's own world of experience and for change in the pupil's world of experience – a balance between have and ought to have?

The Measurement of Reading Ability

The attitude in this book also has consequences for other aspects of elementary reading instruction. If reading is learned as a process of thinking, how can this be tested? How can the pupil's reading ability be measured? In any event, it is not accomplished by oral reading of word lists or meaningless word and sentences. This is illustrated by the fact that a large percentage of young people with reading difficulties will score very low in such tests. Generally they perform poorly in oral reading. Yet if the comprehension they have derived from the text is measured, this is not less than that of normal readers.

132

Do these two groups read alike? Or is their reading different. The formulation of the questions presented to the pupils to measure their reading is important. This is rarely considered in the elaboration of reading tests. It is difficult to do so, for which reason the aspects tested will often be those which are most easily tested.

Do reading tests generally only control the content of the story? Or do they contain questions which allow the pupil to evaluate the content of the text? Do they let the pupil make up his mind regarding the content in relation to his own experiences?

The traditional form of test concept is much too narrow. In fact, a reading test is without meaning if at the same time it is not possible to: 1) test the pupil's ability to find literature, 2) test the pupil's possibilities for using the literature found, and 3) test the pupil's ability to relate this literature to his own experiences. Furthermore the educational materials, teachers and the school in general should be tested in the form of evaluation and description. One should also include the general background of the pupils. *The Test Concept Problem*

Nonetheless, the easy way has generally been chosen, in accordance with test tradition, i. e. testing tiny fragments of reading. These are the parts of reading which are most easily tested and not those which are the most essential and important to reading. Test psychology which proceeds along these fragmentary lines is condemned to fail in a time when one is forced to have interest not in details and casual products of education but in wholes and the entire process.

In the future, more attention will be paid to descriptions of happenings with pupils in the classroom, among their schoolmates, and in their homes. Testing will include aspects of the entire pupil, the teacher, the reading material, and the pupil's ability to find and utilize literature.

The objectives and content of education should direct the testing and not vice versa! The future does not lie in increasing the reliability of testing. On the contrary, the demands of reliability must be released, in order to place more emphasis on validity.

OCCUPATIONAL HAZARD

Yes, he was tempted,
and he fell;
but judge him not
too hard.
It does take character
to sell
elastic
by the yard.

Question 3

How can one change the emphasis from testing of f. ex. unimportant words and sentences to testing of the entire world of the pupil?

A general, and hardly ever reasonable, way of thinking is:

If it is not one thing, then is must be the other; then if it is one thing, it could not be the other as well.

There are very few problems which do not contain considerably more than two alternatives. At the same time they contain a network of mutual causes and effects. What was previously named 'the cause' is simply a concept which cannot always be used. Each single phenomenon cannot be placed in one and only frame of reference. Either-or-ways of thinking may be thinking which blocks reasonable, realistic appraisal.

Perhaps we should now and then think the as-well-as way! Today nobody speaks of the cause of reading difficulties, or of the effect of reading difficulties, or the influence of content on pupils or the effective method.

That is why the fundamental attitude of this book has been that reading is important; in school it is extremely important; but it is not *that* important!

A bit beyond perception's reach
I sometimes believe I see
that Life is two locked boxes, each
containing the other's key.

THE CENTRAL POINT

A philosophistry

I am the Universe's Centre.
No subtle sceptics can confound me;
for how can other viewpoints enter,
when all the rest is all around me?

Scan of the book

Introduction –

*Why Read
This Book
on Reading
Instruction
in Denmark?*

A series of related questions are asked that establish a guideline for an analysis of reading instruction in Denmark, the subject of this book. They are as follows:

Question One – why read this book on reading instruction in Denmark at all?

Question Two – because Denmark may be viewed as a social laboratory where East and West meet?

Question Three – because Denmark is a particular homogeneous society in a tangled world?

Question Four – does the content of this book relate to universal aspects of reading instruction?

Question Five – because Denmark has developed reading methods and extensive reading materials to an astonishing extent for her small language area?

In Denmark issues in reading can be seen through a magnifying glass – methods, materials, elementary reading instruction, individualization of the reader, remedial instruction and advanced reading skills training.

Holistic psychology provides the background for the educational approach to reading. It is an open strategy where reading is considered part of the language. Language development passes through four stages: understanding–listening, listening to speaking, speaking to reading and reading to writing. It is taught according to these four stages, even though functional language involves them all. Yet there are always pupils who 'get the worst of it'. Children, retarded in reading, always exist even when instruction is adequate or good.

Chapter 1 –

A Holistic Educational Approach to Reading

To have one language in a single culture with limited subcultures and one ethnic group has distinct advantages. Danish holistic psychology supports this with the concern about splitting the child and his instruction and with faith in each child's possibilities.

There are many kinds of reading. The ordinary developmental sequence is rebus-reading, transition-reading and content-reading.

Chapter 2 –

Reading Instruction at School

Retarded readers pass through the same stages.

Reading can be viewed as involving various techniques – scanning, skimming, and critical reading. These techniques can be taught but some precautions need to be observed.

Reading instruction is related to various stages of the child's development in school. Formal instructional procedures in the municipal and private kindergartens and in kindergarten class are not recommended. Instruction of children proceeds in a flexible sequence of stages f. ex. for the 6-to-8-year-old, 8-to-10-year-old, 10-to-12-year-old

137

and 11-to-13-year-old. Special attention is given to reading during the last years of elementary school.

The classroom teacher is the teacher of the mother tongue and remains with the same group of children for several years (5–8). Other teacher deal with other learning skills and subject matter – mathematics, science, physical education, foreign language, etc.

Other aspects of language instruction include listening speaking, spelling and creative writing. These are viewed as part of the whole language.

Teaching materials involve typography, language and content. These three aspects are considered in books for rebus-reading, transition-reading and content-reading.

Two different groups of reading retarded children are characterized: 1) the mainly visually reading retarded and 2) the intellectually delayed. Both are impeded by particular linguistic factors.

While most people are content-readers in a literate society (such as Denmark), such people will function at different levels of reading depending on various circumstances. Content may also have various influences on the reader himself.

Chapter 3 –

Remedial Instruction in Reading

About 20 percent of pupils will receive some form of remedial teaching of reading during their schooling from ages 7 through 16. This will vary according to intensity and duration. At any time about five percent of pupils receive special instruction in reading.

Special instruction in reading is recommended by the mother tongue language teacher and the school psychologist. The facilities of the school, classroom teacher, special education teacher, school psychologist and home are utilized in the remediation program that is developed. Remedial instruction follows certain principles and makes use of many methods that consider environments, time and materials. Since the reading retarded are usually successfully integrated into school environments, teachers

138

do not define and demarcate reading retardation in precise ways.

Recognizing the pupil differences, which do exist, and trying to respect these differences during everyday teaching one will encounter large and educationally important problems. In Scandinavia exactly the question of individualization has been an important part of the philosophy of education, one has attempted to carry through.

Chapter 4 –

Individualization and Pupil Differences

The organizational response to such issues and problems in Denmark has been a nine-year non-graded school with small classes and split half classes for certain subjects and on some class levels. These procedures increase the demands for well-trained and highly qualified teachers.

Individualization of pupils goes through individualization of instructional methods and educational materials. Reading tests are minimally used as a basis for the identification of reading retarded pupils and for the design of methods and materials. Individualization is implemented through the pupils' choice from a large variety of materials with different motivating content and containing different educational situations. These situations may involve directive tasks and open tasks.

An example of individualization is illustrated by reading courses for young people and adults in the Royal School of Librarianship. These students select what they think they need to learn among the following possibilities which are taught: speed-reading, skimming, study reading and study problems. The content of these reading courses also reflects individualization principles. The drop-out rate for these absolutely voluntary courses (which give no competence) is less than 10 percent.

Speed-reading courses have existed in some Danish schools for many years and short courses for adults have been increasing but not to the degree that they exist, for example, in the United States. The national Danish tele-

Chapter 5 –

What Speed-Reading Is

vision has provided a limited number of courses for schools and for adults. A psychological conception of what reading is and how reading ability can be improved should be the basis of instruction in speed-reading courses.

Inexpedient explanations of reading deficiencies and ability are examined. They are viewed as signs, symptoms and associated behaviors – visual perception, perceptual span and other single abilities. This is hardly sufficient.

From a holistic point of view reading is something complex – everything that happens within the reader's head when he sees printed symbols and experiences content, thoughts and meaning. The processing of stimuli results in experience of meaning, and the experience of meaning and the processing of stimuli have an interacting influence.

Reading is also determined by other factors such as concurrent voice movements, inner voice and eye regression. Furthermore, the processing of stimuli depends on many other factors within the text and within the reader – the reader's knowledge of what the book is about, the size, content and concepts of the book, the reader's desire to read a certain content, the reader's expectations of the book and the reader's purpose of reading the book.

Speed-reading should be adapted to the purpose of reading. Reading skills training should train different ways of reading corresponding to different purposes.

Chapter 6 –

Principles for Reading Skills Training

Speed reading is more accurately considered reading skills training. A clear statement of objectives is desirable and will affect the content and methods of instruction. There are difficulties in developing objectives because of culturally determined values and conflicts between teacher and student values. A statement of objectives on an individual personality level (techniques, methods, habits, attitudes, motivations, and interests) can be made but these aspects are difficult to measure. At a behavioral level the objectives can be more easily stated and measured – speed in

140

words per minute, comprehension in percentages, changes over times, etc. It is seen as important that the student formulates his or her own objectives and articulate them during the course.

The problem of transfer is a crucial one in all reading and study skill courses. It is often neglected in many reading courses today. The primary aim should be improved reading (variously defined) in daily functioning. In most Danish reading programs transfer is a central part of course content. It includes materials and situations related to and eventually identical with daily work. Reading machines have a minimal role in training.

Again the holistic point of view about reading is emphasized, i. e. reading as a function of the personality. The interaction between reading and other parts of the personality is recognized at the beginning of the reading course as something influencing the reading performance – on a general level as well as quite specifically. And the reading performance also has an effect on feelings, self-esteem etc. The interaction between reading and the *entire* person is evident at a reading course.

Chapter 7 –

Reading Skills Training for Adults – an Individualized Method

A method of reading skills training for adults is designed around individual lessons which can also be adapted to group instruction. A course usually has a structure of nine weeks' duration with 15 minutes of instructional time and two or three hours of independent student training per week. There are three levels of work – self-training, self-evaluation (word counting, rate calculation, reading curve, and weekly reports) and instructional lessons.

The content of the course includes the diagnostic interview, training in books at home following specific instructions, specific forms of training, weekly reports and reading curves and instructional discussions (emphasizing emotional reactions as well as cognitive understanding of problems).

In addition to the initial diagnosis the teacher continues to make diagnostic formulations throughout the course based on weekly instructional discussions. Based on these diagnoses, training prescriptions are developed for the student.

Reading skills training through group instruction follows the principles and procedures of individual lessons. If students do not have a modest knowledge of studying and work habits and the psychology of reading, this is included in the two first lessons. If they have little information about their own reading abilities, this is obtained and discussed. The structure of the course parallels what has been described for individual lessons. Group instruction may have special motivational and social interactional advantages. However, the greatest difficulty is the sufficient consideration of individual differences. Various instructional procedures attempt to accomplish this.

Chapter 8 –

*Reading
Problems
as Described by
Students*

Reading problems can profitably be understood through statements by students of experiences with their own reading. A survey was made on 150 adults who participated in reading skills training courses. Data were obtained from their written reports and from recorded notes of the reading teacher during lessons.

These data were organized into five different categories – technical problems, adapting to new forms of reading, attitudes toward reading, application of new reading skills and work habits and planning. These results have been applied in an illustrative way to the issues of diagnosis and instructional treatment – problem category, typical student statements and suggested treatments.

Chapter 9 –

*Now What?
Some Further
Questions*

This book is based on a holistic point of view in relation to education and to reading in particular. "The Teaching of Reading–without Really Any Method" is really a broad approach to reading.

Reading involves thinking but also has its mechanics.

142

Is it possible to have a theory of reading that integrates thinking and mechanics? Such a view may be utilized in the teaching of reading through the use of reading materials that are related both to the world of experience that a child already has and to the one he ought to have.

Questions can be raised about measures of reading ability particularly from tests. In their traditional form tests are without much meaning; they ignore abilities to find literature, use it and relate it to other literature. They frequently test those small fragments of reading that are easy to handle but not essential to reading. There are many aspects of reading beyond speed such as critical and creative reading and study methods.

Working with advanced reading skills training and study habits means working also with factors that inevitably influence the personality of the individual. Thus an ethical problem arises: Habits and attitudes differ among individuals and determine the ways in which problems other than reading are solved. To what extent may one interfere with the methods of work and the ways of thinking of other human beings? Can methods of teaching be developed that are strong enough to influence cognitive functioning in a durable way and at the same time are varied and adaptable to individual differences?

Either-or -ways of thinking can be replaced by as-well-as forms of thinking. Today few people speak of the cause of or *the* effect of reading difficulties, or *the* influence of content or the effective method.

In conclusion, reading is important; in school it is extremely important; but it is not that important!

This is the fundamental and basic attitude of this book.

Some facts about Denmark.
Educational system and language

Size

Today Denmark is a 'State of Danes' distributed over an area of 16,619 square miles. The population is about 5 million.

Government

Denmark is a kingdom, since 1972 ruled by Queen Margrethe II.

Through two generations Denmark has been governed mainly by Social Democrats ("The Danish Labor Party") usually supported by urban intellectuals and small rural property holders. During the last ten years, however, there has been greater political mobility than earlier. The stability traditionally characterizing the Scandinavian democracies, is no longer characteristic.

As regards foreign affairs and defense policy, Denmark is a member of NATO, an arrangement supported by a significant part of the Danish voters. In 1972 the country joined the European Economic Community. However, Denmark still might be considered one of the less European-minded of the countries in the Common Market.

Economy

Agriculture, which was formerly the main commodity of trade, now employs a little less than 10 percent of the population and sells most of its production abroad. Danish farm work is highly mechanized. Agricultural export consists of butter, cheese, milk, bacon, eggs, meat, pork, vegetables and beer.

About 40 percent of the population are employed in

Figure 17

service occupations. The remaining 50 percent are employed in industry and trades.

Industry is based on easy access to the import of raw materials and fuel. Industrial exports consist of machines, ships, canned foods, textiles, electronic instruments, furniture, concrete, pharmaceutical products, chemicals, etc.

145

The import surplus is hopefully balanced by earnings from foreign trade and tourism.

Currency is based on 1 krone of 100 øre. One American dollar is equivalent to about 6 kr. and one British pound is equivalent to about 10 kr. (December, 1977).

Religion

By far most Danes belong to the State Lutheran Church; however, there is complete religious freedom.

Social Conditions and Education

When measured by an international yardstick, differences in cultural level are *very* small within Denmark.

Nevertheless, in actual practice, social conditions in Denmark do create some limiting factors. For instance it cannot be claimed that everybody in the country can obtain optimum education. A prosperous community is not necessarily a welfare state. In particular, interest in education varies. When urban areas are compared with rural districts, eliminating some higher income groups, people in rural districts probably are somewhat less interested in at least *higher* education than those in urban areas. One of the contributing factors may be the lack of tradition for and interest in academic training among the rural population. This phenomenon is receiving increasing public attention and changes are likely to occur within the next decade.

Social barriers arising from family background play a far greater role in the seeking of education than do geographical barriers or degree of urbanization (Hansen, 1972). This would create great imbalance, were it not equalized by a well-developed further educational system and inservice training facilities, which are provided in almost all parts of the country.

In principle the cost of all tuition for children and young people, including all educational materials, is provided by public funds. For more current social and educational statistics, the official national statistics should be referred to.

146

In many of the industrial areas in Denmark the kinder- *The Kinder-*
garten has become a necessity for children from three to *garten*
seven years of age due to both parents' employment outside the home. In modern times the establishment of kindergartens is considered a community responsibility. The
kindergartens can accommodate 30 percent of the children in this age group (1976). Although there is no need
for kindergarten facilities to cover the entire remaining
percentage, the overall capacity is far from sufficient.

The kindergarten admits children from three to seven
years old. During the week it is open from three to ten
hours daily. Its aim is to provide children with security
and stimulation, irrespective of their home environments
and their parents' occupational level and abilities as educators. The Danish kindergarten is more than a playground or a placement service for the children. It is a
learning workshop, where children can develop motor,
intellectual, linguistic and other abilities – but not in
any formal way; social development is strongly emphasized.

It is a place where children, gradually and in pace
with their personal development, may gain experience in
the normal requirements of the community in which they
live: standards of everyday living, working life, social life,
conventional behaviors, mass media, art and creative subjects. One specific aim of the kindergarten is to provide
experience from which young children can learn to respect other people and to evoke their respect. Such a
kindergarten is not a preschool institution, formally training children for school.

Many people consider the kindergarten class in school a *The Kinder-*
natural outgrowth of kindergarten principles. The kin- *garten Class*
dergarten class is accommodated in the public school. It *and Starting*
is open about three hours a day, and its purpose is to *School*
promote the motor, social, cognitive, emotional and creative development of 6-year-old children. The kinder-

147

garten classes cover about 50 percent of the children of this age. It is often said that the kindergarten class is a preparation for school proper. While part of the costs in kindergarten must be paid for by the parents, the school kindergarten is free, in line with the free public education policy.

In comparison with some other countries, entry into first grade in Denmark is at a rather late age: the calendar year in which the child is 7 years old, with the possibility of starting one year earlier or one year later. Although it is anticipated that parents during the coming years may demand more opportunities for their children to obtain education at an earlier age, there is no indication that generally they would desire formal instruction at an earlier level. On the contrary, politicians, educators and parents are generally agreed that an earlier start in school should be devoted to the creative and imaginative experiences currently provided in kindergarten and preschool classes.

The Public School System

The compulsory period of education in Denmark is nine years. In practice ten years is the usual for most pupils. The public school is owned and administered by the local municipality, which receives a refund from the State for all essential expenses and is supervised by central and regional educational authorities.

It should be mentioned, however, that there is a growing risk of rather high differences as the local councils now allocate the amounts for education within the framework given by governmental circulars.

The 1975 parliamentary act governing the primary and lower secondary schools defines the structure of the school and the main subjects of its curriculum. "... The object of folkeskolen is – in co-operation with the parents – to give the pupils a possibility of acquiring knowledge, skills, working methods, and ways of expressing them-

148

selves which will contribute to the all-round development of the individual pupil.

(2) In all of its work, folkeskolen shall attempt to create such possibilities of experience and self-expression that the pupils may increase their desire to learn, expand their imagination, and develop their ability to making independent assessments, evaluations and opinions.

(3) Folkeskolen shall prepare the pupils for taking an active interest in their environment and for participation in decision making in a democratic society, and for a share in the responsibility for the solution of common tasks. Consequently, teaching and the entire daily life must be based on intellectual liberty and democracy."

By an international comparison it might be noticed that there are almost as many female as male teachers in elementary school; however, for the time being the recruitment of female teachers is larger. There is to some extent a larger number of female teachers for mother tongue instruction and during the first years of school; this corresponds to more male teachers of mathematics and during the last years of school. Reasons for these facts cannot be given with any high degree of certainty.

It may be practical to keep in mind the age of Danish students on various class levels. (See also page 34).

Figure 18

Student's age:	
Grade	Age
1	7– 8
2	8– 9
3	9–10
4	10–11
above 4	11–16

The Danish Language

Danish is spoken by approximately 5 million Danes living in Denmark. It is also spoken in the Faroe Islands where there is a population of about 40,000. The Faroese

149

children are taught Danish from their third year of school. Part of their education is also conducted in Danish.

In Greenland, which is a separate administrative area of Denmark, the Greenland language is spoken by over 40,000 people. Children are taught the Greenland language from their first years of school. Danish teaching starts in the third grade. The objectives of the school are very similar to those of the Danish school. A majority of the teachers are Danish.

In Iceland, Danish is now the first foreign language and is taught from grade 4. English is the second foreign language. In parts of their education after elementary school, books in Danish and English are used. Danish literature is very much read in Iceland, including magazines, comic books and, to a limited extent, newspapers.

South of Denmark there is a minority population in Schleswig (Sydslesvig), which is part of the German Federal Republic (West Germany), of about 40,000 people who speak Danish. About 6,000 children attend Danish schools and about 1,800 attend Danish kindergartens. In these Danish schools the children are taught Danish first and foremost, but also German to a high degree. In principle their education in German must be of a quality corresponding to that of other schools in West Germany. In addition to the 40,000 Danish-speaking people there are about 5,000 pro-Danish, who are German-speaking. – Furthermore, in the southern part of Denmark there are about 12,000 pro-German Danes who are German-speaking. They have their own mainly German-speaking schools with about 1,600 pupils.

Books and libraries in Denmark.

Through many years book promotion in Denmark has been a constant activity and concern of professional circles. Cooperation has been established between publishers, booksellers and libraries to ensure the best conditions possible for the general distribution of books. For example, a common cataloguing service operates to promote reading habits. Government grants are available to a few authors and fewer translators to support creative work. Authors are provided compensation by the government for public lending rights through libraries.

Statistics on Books

A few statistics may serve as illustration. In a population of five million, about 7,100 book titles are published annually of which approximately 5,100 are original works and approximately 2,000 are translations. Books are on sale at about 700 booksellers all over the country and on loan in about 1,200 public libraries and library branches, easily accessible to everybody, and a network of bookmobiles operate, especially in the rural areas. School libraries are compulsory in all public schools.

The stocks of public libraries are about 25 million volumes and about 65 million books are borrowed from libraries annually. To this should be added professional libraries at universities and institutes of higher education.

Public Library Lendings

Figure 19 illustrates the number of book lendings to adults and children from public libraries each year from 1959 through 1977. Loans to children show a remarkable increase from 1969 to 1970. This finding might be the result of the more child-centered attitude of children's libraries. In addition, a newly oriented teaching of the

151

mother tongue language (Danish) was introduced in the elementary school in 1960–1961. Probably this teaching is slowly being reflected in increased book lendings since 1967–1968.

Book Lendings From School Libraries

In addition to public library lendings it should be noted that book lendings from school libraries have also increased proportionally. The annual lendings from school libraries show the following.

1968/69	10,394,000
1969/70	13,581,000
1970/71	17,757,000
1971/72	21,561,000
1972/73	25,221,000
1973/74	27,242,000
1974/75	29,477,000
1975/76	32,224,000

Before 1968/69 it is not possible to obtain more than approximate figures.

Book Lendings from Other School Sources

However, these data do not cover the facts completely. Many schools have even larger lendings of especially easy books to be used by children with reading problems. These books are distributed in large numbers from reading clinics and small book storerooms at the school. In addition most schools have some classroom-sets and solitary books directly administered by the deputy chief of the school. These books are part of the ordinary collection of materials of the schools and are not administered by the school librarian.

The specific data on library lendings indicated above should be treated with reservation. They are approximate figures and are probably too low. In spite of this it is quite clear that the lending of books to children of school age has increased enormously within the last decade. When this finding is related to the general increase in

152

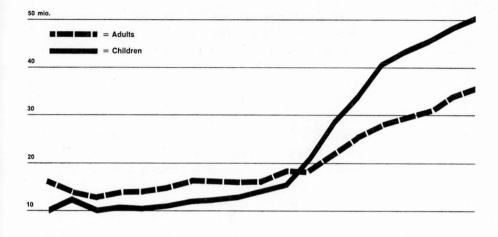

50 mio.

■ ■■ ■■ ■ = Adults

■■■■■■■■ = Children

40

30

20

10

59/60 ˙ 60/61 ˙ 61/62 ˙ 62/63 ˙ 63/64 ˙ 64/65 ˙ 65/66 ˙ 66/67 ˙ 67/68 ˙ 68/69 ˙ 69/70 ˙ 70/71 ˙ 71/72 ˙ 72/73 ˙ 73/74 ˙ 74/75 ˙ 75/76 ˙ 76/77 ˙

Figure 19

lending of books and purchase of books of the entire population, the phenomenon is striking indeed! It should also be mentioned that the number of bestselling Danish children's books printed corresponds to the number printed of common children's books in some of the larger Western language areas. Compared to the population, the Danish number printed is rather high.

The Growth of Books for the Reading Retarded

In addition to general children's books, books and other reading material for the reading retarded have been emphasized. In this field there has been an extraordinarily vigorous development during the last 25 years. When Danish educational materials for the reading retarded are compared with foreign educational materials for similar groups of pupils, it is striking how much the Danish materials emphasize the quality of the contents and the motivating aspects and how little emphasis is placed on formal exercises.

153

During the years from 1952 to 1976 it was possible to produce a wide selection of such reading materials. A summary of materials was recommended by a broadly composed committee of reading teachers as usable for the instruction of reading retarded. It contained a total of 475 books and other materials for various types of special reading training. About 40 materials were available for writing training in the mother tongue language (Lundahl, 1969). The two corresponding figures in 1952 were about 60 and 30 respectively (Larsen, 1952).

Since 1969 two further lists have been added: "List of materials and free reading texts for the teaching of Danish in grades 1–7 and special reading training. 175 easy books for young people and adults" (Lundahl, 1975), and "List of easy professional reading and manuals in the class" with about 800 titles (Lundahl, 1976). These lists were chosen from an even remarkably higher number of titles than was the case in 1952. In 1952 it was thought that such a list could be used for many years, but now it is revised every second year as a routine.

Furthermore in 1952 usable reading materials might have been placed on a dining table without much difficulty. More by luck than by intention these materials had acceptable content in an acceptable form of presentation. A list of effective materials for special reading and writing training could not possibly have been worked out at that time.

Even though there is very little overlapping of the lists in 1952 and in 1976, the increase of materials for the reading retarded from less than 100 to well over 1,500 tells something about the development which has been going on for more than two decades in a language area of about five million inhabitants. One is now starting a production of books and tape recordings for the most severely reading retarded among individuals with a variety of handicaps – brain damaged, intellectually retarded, etc.

APPENDIX C

Content analysis of children's books and educational materials

During the last decade there has been much interest in analyzing the content of books and other educational materials at the disposal of children. Analysis of basal readers has been done to determine among other things how the pattern of society has been reflected in their content.

Critical Analysis of Educational Materials

There also has been much specific interest in viewing the pattern of sex-roles through the looking-glass of primer stories. In the recent past one did get the impression that female members in the "ABC" families were mostly portrayed in distinctly domestic situations and apparently only in week-ends. The books have decidedly changed, but criticism still remains.

The criticism has been raised in other countries that national and ethnic minorities do not appear in children's books and school books, or at any rate, not in reasonably 'honest' descriptions. Such minorities have little actuality in Denmark.

Many of these studies are motivated by genuine resentment and much indignation. Now and then there is so much resentment and indignation that the results were obtained before the start of the study. In these instances the studies have just been a delaying intermediate stage before the publishing of results and conclusions.

Comments on the Motivation of Those Who Perform Analyses

The attitude a person has before starting the counting of illustrations, situations, semantic terms, etc., that are related to the pattern of sex-roles, the pattern of society

	Illustrations of Men				Illustrations of Women				Illustrations of Boys				Illustrations of Girls				
	A	B	C	D	A	B	C	D	A	B	C	D	A	B	C	D	
Material 1	45	42	49	45	8	12	4	8	98	101	105	100	93	89	70	91	960
Material 2	28	26	32	30	20	21	14	19	105	92	109	104	90	90	68	92	940
Material 3	43	40	45	42	23	20	18	24	135	120	132	132	102	97	87	102	1162
Total	116	108	126	117	51	53	36	51	338	313	346	336	285	276	225	285	3062

Figure 20

or other matters has a great, and probably often over-looked, significance. This can be illustrated by a book that was surveyved by four different people, A–D, figure 20.

One person is a member of a women's liberation group whose aim is to demonstrate the masculine dominance in society. A second person is a man very much engaged in social problems, who readily agrees with women's lib-eration in words and attitude, though hardly in action ac-cording to his female friend. A third person is a female secretary in a publishing firm; she is very much engaged in social problems, but is consciously trying to place her-self at a certain distance from the women's liberation group; she views their actions as destroying the chance for a change in the society pattern which she also desires. A fourth person is one of the authors of the book in question who had done a content analysis (Jansen, to be published).

All four persons were asked to describe the distribution of males and females! The different results in the four countings may be explained by the fact among others that the member of the women's liberation group counted snow-men, pixies (as long as they did not appear in skirts), wooden men and most dogs and cats as males. Even though the results of this analysis were extreme, it is still remarkable how the three other analyses differed –

156

and it was not a question of "miscalculation" but of different interpretations of persons appearing in the great number of illustrations in the material in question.

Perhaps this provides a suggestion that to perform content analyses is more complicated than many who do such analyses realize.

An extensive analysis of the content of *all* Danish books for mother tongue instruction from the first through the seventh year of school was performed by experienced and professionally qualified people (teachers and psychologists). This was done during the last period of the sixties and revealed a number of facts regarding authors, world geography and the age period when the story was written. These Danish readers included texts written by "real" authors and did not include basal readers.

An Extensive
Analysis
of Content of
Danish Readers

Rank	Name	Sex	Country	Frequency
1.	Andersen, Hans Christian	M	Denmark	109
2.	Rasmussen, Halfdan	M	Denmark	89
3.	Aakjær, Jeppe	M	Denmark	45
4.	Grundtvig, N. F. S.	M	Denmark	39
5.	Aesop's fables	M	Greece	38
6.	Bjørnson, Bjørnstjerne	M	Norway	34
7.	Jensen, Johannes V.	M	Denmark	33
11.	Egner, Thorbjørn	M	Norway	28
12.	Grimm, Jacob and W. G.	M	Germany	27
14.	Lindgren, Astrid	F	Sweden	22
18.	Lagerlöf, Selma	F	Sweden	17
25.	Kipling, Rudyard	M	England	13
28.	Topelius, Zacharias	M	Finland	13
29.	Asbjørnsen, P. Chr. & Moe	M	Norway	12
37.	Wessel, Johan Herman	M	Norway	11
42.	Münchhausen, K. F.	M	Germany	10
45.	Gunnarsson, Gunnar	M	Iceland	9
51.	Grieg, Nordahl	M	Norway	8

157

55. Wilder, Laura Ingalls	F	USA	8
62. Twain, Mark	M	USA	7
64. Zetterström, Hasse	M	Sweden	7
66. Brisley, Joyce L.	F	England	6
71. la Fontaine, Jean de	M	France	6
72. Milne, A. A.	M	England	6
75. Tetzner, Lisa	F	Germany	6
76. Vestly, Anne Cath.	F	Norway	6

Authors who Were Represented

Here 26 authors are mentioned. The other authors among the 26 most frequently represented are Scandinavian and not known in other countries.

The Danish author, Hans Christian Andersen, was most frequently represented. After that there was a gap between him and other Danish authors: a lyric poet of our time, Halfdan Rasmussen, (children's poems); Jeppe Aakjær who has written a great deal of regional poetry; and a hymn poet, N. F. S. Grundtvig, who has also written some patriotic songs.

In fifth rank was, quite astonishingly, Aesop's fables. The Norwegian poet, Bjørnstjerne Bjørnson and the Danish Nobel Prize winner Johannes V. Jensen followed. The author represented in eleventh rank was a Norwegian poet, Thorbjørn Egner. Number twelve was the Grimm brothers' (Germans) with folktales, and number fourteen, the Swedish author of children's books, Astrid Lindgren. Number eighteen is the Swedish author, Selma Lagerlöf, also a Nobel Prize winner.

The first poet from the English-speaking world was Kipling, also a Nobel Prize winner, number 25. A Finnish author, Zacharias Topelius, who has written historical stories and children's books, was equally represented, and so were the Norwegian 'collectors of folktales', Asbjørnsen and Moe.

Among the total of 76 authors most frequently represented in Danish readers there were also others from foreign countries. These included Johan Herman Wessel of Norway, Münchhausen of Germany, Gunnar Gunnarsson of Iceland, Nordahl Grieg and Anne Cath. Vestly of Norway, Laura Ingalls Wilder and Mark Twain of the US, Hasse Zetterström of Sweden, Joyce Brisley and A. A. Milne (Winnie the Pooh!) of England, Jean de la Fontaine of France, and Lisa Tetzner of Germany.

Regarding the sex of the above mentioned authors, there were 65 men and 11 women. If this is compared with the actual distribution of authors according to sex, the distributions are practically identical. *Sex of the Authors*

The total number of pages, standardized as 1,700 letters/page, for each country in the entire sample of books was counted. This number was placed on a standard geographic world map. Then the number of standardized pages of all Danish textbooks in the sample was equaled to its actual geographical area. Other countries were then related to the Danish geographical area by their proportional number of pages in relation to Denmark. This was represented on a world map (figure 21). *The World as Presented by Children's Books*

From the viewpoint of Danish readers, Denmark makes up a very large part of the world. The other Scandinavian countries, especially Norway and Sweden, with which Denmark traditionally has strong relations, are also an essential part of the world. The Catholic parts of the world and the 'technically under-developed countries' are strongly underrepresented. Africa is somewhat an exception. This may be explained by the fact that a Danish author (Karen Blixen) often took her motives from Africa, and – to a higher extent – that African folktales form part of many collections of fairytales.

Samples of Norwegian, English, American, and French books showed that Danish readers were strikingly *less* nationally centered than readers from these countries - - -.

It was possible to rate the time period during which most of the stories were written. They were rated according to the following groups: *Time Period*

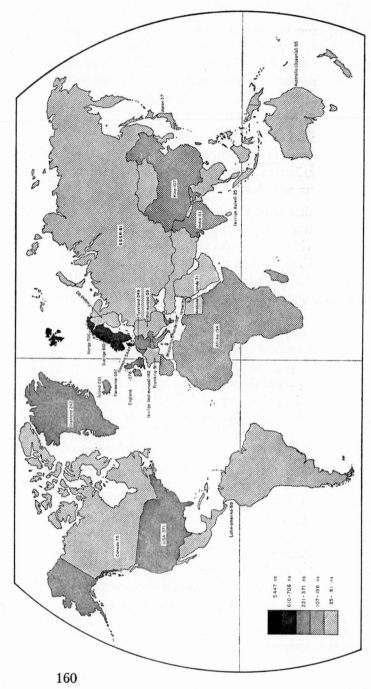

160

Figure 21 A

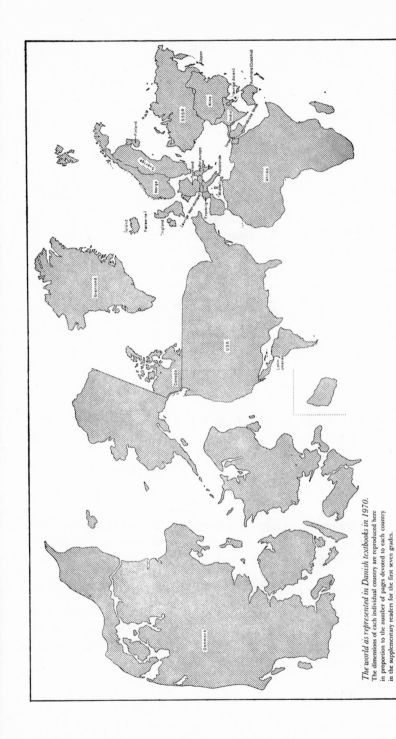

The world as represented in Danish textbooks in 1970.
The dimensions of each individual country are reproduced here
in proportion to the number of pages devoted to each country
in the supplementary readers for the first seven grades.

Figure 21 B

Figure 22

a.	unclassified	N = 125
b.	folktales	N = 250
c.	earlier than the year 200	N = 40
d.	years 200–1100	N = 10
e.	years 1100–1499	N = 60
f.	1500's	N = 10
g.	1600's	N = 20
h.	1700's	N = 50
i.	years 1800–1819	N = 50
j.	years 1820–1839	N = 125
k.	years 1840–1869	N = 250
l.	years 1870–1899	N = 130
m.	years 1900–1919	N = 230
n.	years 1920–1929	N = 180
o.	years 1930–1939	N = 175
p.	years 1940–1945	N = 340
r.	years 1946–1950	N = 175
s.	years 1951–1956	N = 415
t.	years 1957–1960	N = 260
u.	years 1961–	N = 320

As can be seen from this table there was a striking number of stories written in the time period 1951–1956. These textbooks were published close to the time when the texts were written. Other large figures in Figure 22 give a hint of (by the way, well-known) culminating points of Nordic literature. On the whole, the distribution shows that a large number of books used in reading relate to a time prior to modern times. An emphasis on tradition and history is very much in evidence.

Representation of Minorities and Environments

In Danish readers it is striking that the handicapped as a minority are mentioned very little. On the other hand the only national minority, Greenlanders, appear in even much larger numbers than might be expected considering their actual small number.

162

Within the borders of Denmark, there is an under-representation of the capital and certain parts of the country. Looking at environments which are described, they seem rather scattered. In the basal readers, there is a decided overemphasis on middle class environments. In other readers the emphasis systematically reflects the literature of the country.

Looking at the geographic regions presented across the borders in Danish readers, Central Europe (represented especially by Germany) appeared relatively frequently until 1940. After this year there was a dramatic fall during World War II: 1939–45. After 1945 English and Swedish references replaced the former Central European emphasis. The French-speaking world is referred to in a very limited extent in content. This is also a reflection of a general Danish interest in contacts above the Danish border during the same period.

Geographic Representation from a Historical Viewpoint

Content analysis of primers, readers, exercise books and textbook material on the written language has also dealt with the educational activities presented in the books; for example:

Analysis of Educational Content

1. Are the questions stated with or without specific response categories?

2. What kinds of exercises are presented?

3. Are there phonetic exercises in the books?

4. Are pupils encouraged to read orally and silently with control, limited control or without control?

The Danish Institute for Educational Research has done these types of analysis of content since the 1960's. The only reports on these studies in English are the English summaries in a number of reports (Jansen, 1966, 1969, and Jansen & Ahm, 1971). Examples of Danish as a foreign language are given in Jansen (1975).

APPENDIX D

National television programs in reading instruction

The experiences in Denmark with the use of television as a teaching instrument for a large number of people in reading skills training has been in the process of development for five years. At the end of the 1960's a school tele-teaching program was worked out and telecasted to pupils from the 7th to 10th year of school. It was repeated later in an improved version. Then a tele-teaching program for the ordinary adult population was introduced; this program was also repeated later. Each of the two original television programs were studied through research projects.

School Television Project

The reading skills training program of the school television project consisted of four telecasts of 20 minutes' duration distributed over seven weeks. In the later version there were six telecasts. These were supported by a set of materials consisting of the pupil's booklet, three reading tests and a questionnaire plus a teacher's booklet.

The goal was to teach pupils how to read faster and more flexibly. The program series was followed by a little more than 8,000 pupils from 7th to 10th year of school; they worked with the program during class lessons at school. To nearly all pupils and to most teachers the topic was unfamiliar. In a way the series functioned as training of teachers in a new educational medium.

The training was non-mechanical. Its major principle was teaching pupils how to read faster by applying special instructions to a series of easy to read books. The

164

telecasts consisted of demonstrations, instructions and illustrative interviews.

In a Copenhagen suburban municipality the director of school research, Jesper Florander, made a study of the effects of the school television program (Florander, 1970). The main purpose of the study was to find out if short-term and long-term effects of the reading speed training could be demonstrated. Attitudes and opinions about the programs were obtained from pupils and teachers.

Evaluation of the Project

The study included a test group of 15 classes with a total of 338 pupils and a control group of 14 classes with a total of 320 pupils. Reading tests were done before and during the series of telecasts and immediately after their termination. Further retesting was performed about four months following the completion of the series. Standard reading tests and special reading tests, designed especially for this purpose, were used.

The study demonstrated a noticeable short-term effect from reading training with highly significant differences in the progress of reading speed within the two groups. A long-term effect was also ascertained. Reading comprehension did not seem to change during the entire period. A large majority of teachers and pupils stated that "they would gladly follow a reading training course once again or advise others to do so."

The tele-teaching program for adults, like the school program, was probably the first of its kind in Europe. There were also very few published experiences from the United States.

Adult Tele-Project

The series consisted of eight weekly telecasts each lasting 20–25 minutes and of a set of materials including a textbook, two questionnaires and 10 reading tests. The series was announced on television and in newspapers. A little more than 10,000 persons ordered the set of materials and were, consequently, counted as participants in the teaching. Several times more people (about a quarter of a million) were acquainted with the topic to a certain extent by watching some of the telecasts.

The aim of the series was that after the course the participants should be able to (1) read faster, (2) read more flexibly, and (3) skim. The series was aimed at a large group of 'ordinary' adult readers who wished to read better, were prepared to follow the telecasts and work in between them. It was emphasized that the course was not for reading retarded people or for study techniques.

Like the school television programs, the participants used self-chosen books in training, a very essential aspect. However, the participants did not have a group for support during the difficult process of training. This placed heavy demands on the motivating qualities of the telecasts.

Content of
Telecasts

The content of the eight telecasts could be divided into three different form categories:

(1) Part of the time was used for direct instruction by the television-teacher on the screen or the television-teacher with text demonstrations and illustrations on the tv-screen. These instructions included what was to be worked with before the next time (a repeated item), how to use a speedcard (cf. page 99), how to skim, and similar subjects.

(2) Another part of the time was used for communication of background knowledge with the aid of pictures, films, demonstrations and illustrations. Topics and problems were presented, such as reading speed, regressions, bad habits when reading, reading and noise, work inhibitions, motivation, vocabulary and the inner voice.

(3) A third part of the time was used for group conversations and interviews. A study group of six participants, selected as representatives of various professions,

166

age and sex, was present at all the broadcasts. They discussed their results, difficulties, ways of solving training problems and reactions to reading training as a whole. This activity was employed to support and motivate the viewers working alone all over the country.

The textbook contained an introductory article of a surveying and motivating character, eight summaries to be read after the telecasts and a thorough alphabetical reading dictionary with explanations of professional words and forms of training used in the program. *The Textbook*

Of the 10 reading tests, seven were fiction and reasonably comparable in degree of difficulty. Three of the reading tests were professional tests, their contents being taken from the teaching of reading from the psychology and sociology of reading. One reading test was to be used in relation to each telecast. Two other tests were available for optional use. *Reading Tests*

The two questionnaires consisted of a series of questions on reading skills, habits and attitudes. They were designed to assist in self-evaluation and in the analysis of one's own reading situation. They were filled in at certain times during the program. *Questionnaires*

Participants were expected to perform many activities independently. This included watching the telecasts, reading the textbook and doing the weekly reading test. They were instructed in choosing literary training material and in training with this material for 30–45 minutes four days a week. Personally adapted training forms were employed. Weekly reports and reading curves of their training were kept. The program series was based on self activity and learning by doing rather than usual tele-teaching, where the teacher is supposed to "teach the pupil the subject."

167

Two questionnaire studies were aimed at a systematic evaluation of the program series and a clarification of some issues related to its use (Jacobsen, 1971). The main purpose of the first study was to find out the characteristics of those people participating in the instruction and how these participants evaluated the outcome for themselves.

Two hundred randomly drawn participants received one questionnaire at the start of the series and another questionnaire at termination. The first questionnaire was answered by 82.5 percent. A little less than one fourth had dropped out by the time of termination. The termination questionnaire was answered by 58.2 percent. An analysis of the first questionnaires was made as well as the background information on the respondents.

In the group of participants there was a considerable preponderance of men (78.5 percent). The distribution in occupational groups showed that a little less than half the participants were employees. Approximately one fourth of the participants were highly educated. These findings were much higher than those for the population as a whole. The geographical distribution of the participants did not correspond to the general population. There were more participants from the capital and less from rural districts. However, the percentage from town areas was similar to that of the country.

In the first questionnaire the participants were asked, what led to their participation in the course. Most of the participants answered that it was the wish to read faster or to do more reading. They were very unsatisfied with their own reading speed and with their ability to skim. However, they were satisfied with their understanding of reading. These results indicated that the participants were indeed those at whom the course was directed.

At the end of the course many participants stated that their reading speed had increased. Correspondingly definitive progress in reading speed was noted from the first to the last reading test. However, reasons for this progress were not systematically examined.

Other participants progressed in other areas. It is interesting that each participant seemed to have had his own special benefit qualitatively different from others. One person learned how to skim, another how to sort out materials and still another person increased his interest in reading.

Nearly half of the participants strongly recommended the series in case it might be repeated. Half of the participants referred to the program with favor.

Thus, the overall evaluation of the course was positive or moderate.

From the data of this study it was possible to calculate the relation between the progress in reading speed expected by the participants at the start of the course and the actual progress finally obtained. There was a notable correspondence between expectation and actualization.

The main purpose of the second study was to obtain a systematic evaluation of the various parts of the telecasts and the materials. Other questions were also clarified. A weekly evaluation form was sent to the 200 randomly selected participants. Through this form it was possible to illustrate various aspects of drop-outs throughout the course. Some of the participants declared in the forms that they had dropped out. This number increased steadily through the weeks reaching a maximum of nearly one fourth. When these figures were compared with the number of completely unanswered forms, it was possible to estimate how many and where drop-outs occurred during the course. Of 200 sample participants, there were between 61.5 and 86 percent who followed the course a little more than half way, until the fifth telecast. A number between 46.5 and 78.5 percent completed the course.

Second Study –
Drop-out Rate

169

References*

Björnsson, C. H. *Läsbarhet*. (Readability.) Stockholm: Liber, 1968.

Blom, G. E., S. G. Zimet & J. L. Wiberg. Attitudes and values in primers from the United States and twelve other countries. In: S. G. Zimet (Ed.) *What children read in school. Critical analysis of primary reading textbooks*. New York & London: Grune & Stratton. 1972.

Braam, L. S. & A. Berger. Effectiveness of four methods of increasing reading rate, comprehension and flexibility. *Journal of Reading*, 1968, *11*, 346–352.

Bredsdorff, A. The children's library service in Denmark. In Coldwell, E. (Ed.), *Library service to children*, volume 1. 2nd revised edition. Lund: Bibliotekstjänst, 1965.

Brickman, W. *Denmark's educational system and problems*. Washington, D. C.: U.S. Department of Health, Education and Welfare, Office of Education, 1967.

Causey, O. S. & J. A. Fischer. Transfer techniques in reading laboratory work. *Journal of Developmental Reading*, 1959, *2*, 3–10.

Cramer, I. Training of children's librarians in Denmark. In Bredsdorff, A. (Ed.), *Library service to children*, 3. Training. Copenhagen: Bibliotekscentralen, 1970.

Danmarks Statistik. Statistisk årbog 1976. (Yearbook of statistics, 1976.) Copenhagen: Danmarks Statistik, 1976 (with English index).

Dewey, J. *How we think*. Boston, Mass.: Heat and Co., 1910.

Dewey, J. *Democracy and education*. New York: McMillan, 1916.

Downing, J. *Comparative Reading*. New York: MacMillan, 1973.

Edfeldt, Å. W. *Att läsa*. (To read.) Stockholm: Svenska Bokförlaget, 1968. p. 24.

Florander, J. Udbyttet af læsetræning. (The effect of the school television program in speed-reading.) Offprint of *Læsepædagogen*, 1970, *18*(2).

From, F. *Perception of other people*. New York: Columbia University Press, 1971. p. 72–86.

Gray, W. S. & B. Rogers. *Maturity in reading. Its nature and appraisal.* Chicago: University of Chicago Press, 1956.

Hansen, E. J. *De 14–20 åriges uddannelsessituation 1965. I. Social og geografisk rekruttering.* (The educational situation of Danish youth of 14 to 20 years in 1965. Vol. I. Social and geographical origin.) Copenhagen: The Danish National Institute of Social Research, 1968. Publication no. 31. (With English abstract and English summary).

Hansen, E. J. *Lighed gennem uddannelse?* (Equality through education?) Copenhagen: The Danish National Institute of Social Research, 1972. Pamphlet no. 1.

International Reading Association. Code of ethics. *The Reading Teacher,* 1969, *22,* 460.

Jacobsen, B. *Evaluering af undervisningsserien læsetræning for voksne. I–II.* (Evaluation of the educational series "Reading improvement for adults in tv".) Copenhagen: Danmarks Radio, 1971.

Jacobsen, B., M. Jansen, I. Kettner & F. Lundahl. *Læsetræning for voksne i tv.* (Training of reading skills for adults in tv.) Copenhagen: Danmarks Radio, 1971.

Jacobsen, B., M. Jansen & F. Lundahl. *Læsekursus, Metodisk vejledning.* (Reading course. Teacher's guide.) Copenhagen: Munksgaard, 1972.

Jakobsen, G. (Ed.). *Dansk Lix 70.* (Danish Lix 70.) Readability index. Copenhagen: Læsepædagogen, 1970 (a)

Jakobsen, G. *Training course for school librarians. Course guide.* Copenhagen: The Royal Danish School of Educational Studies, 1970.

Jakobsen, G. Teaching children's literature in the teacher's colleges in Denmark. *Bookbird,* 1971. *9*(4), 20–27.

Jakobsen, G. Research in children's literature in Denmark. *Internationales Symposium für Kinder- und Jugend Litteratur. Vom 18. bis 22. Oktober 1971 in Frankfurt am Main.* (International symposium on children's literature.) Frankfurt a.M.: Klaus Doderer, 1972.

Jakobsen, G. (Ed.). *Dansk Lix 75.* (Danish Lix 75.) Readability index Copenhagen: Læsepædagogen, 1975.

Jansen, M. *Special- og begynderundervisning i dansk.* (Special and beginners' instruction in Danish.) Copenhagen: Læsepædagogen, 1959.

Jansen, M. The scope of reading in Scandinavia. In Jenkinson, M. D. (Ed.), *Reading instruction: An international forum.* Newark, Del.: IRA, 1966.

Jansen, M. *Skriftligt arbejde i dansk 1.–7. skoleår.* Registrering og analyse af bøger til undervisningen i skriftlig dansk. (Registration and analysis of textbook material used in grades 1–7 in the teaching of written Danish.) Copenhagen: The Danish Institute for Educational Research, 1966. No. 60. (with English summary).

Jansen, M. *How long will we go on waiting for "the Great Pumpkin"?* Copenhagen: The Danish Institute for Educational Research, 1968. (Duplicated). Paper read at the Second World Congress on Reading in Copenhagen 1968. Also in German translation.

Jansen, M. *Danske læsebøger 1.–7. skoleår.* I del. Registrering og analyse. II del. Forfatter- og titelregister. (Danish readers grades 1–7. Part I. Registration and analysis. Part II. Bibliography.) Copenhagen: The Danish Institute for Educational Research, 1969. No. 70 (with English summary).

Jansen, M. *Teaching of reading – without specific methods? On the teaching of reading in Denmark.* Copenhagen: The Danish Institute for Educational Research, 1970. Report no. 1.

Jansen, M. Læsestof til de svage læsere. (Reading materials for retarded readers.) *Bogen i skolen,* 1971, 7(2), 3–18.

Jansen, M. *555 lærerskemaer analyseret med hensyn til klasselærerarbejdet, fag m. v.* (555 teacher-schedules analyzed with regard to the work of the classroom-teacher, subjects, etc.) Copenhagen: 1973 (Duplicated).

Jansen, M. The languages of Denmark. In: Downing, J. (Ed.), *Comparative Reading.* Cross-National studies of behavior and processes in reading and writing. New York: The Macmillan Company, 1973. Offprint.

Jansen, M. *Fremmedsprogs- og modersmålsundervisning – belyst gennem empirisk undersøgelse, hvor danskundervisning i Island er fulgt via undervisningsiagttagelser.* (Teaching of foreign language and mother tongue examined through an empiric investigation of Danish teaching in Iceland.) Den statistiske analyse i bog II i samarbejde med Svend Kreiner Møller. Copenhagen: Munksgaard, 1975. Danmarks pædagogiske Institut. No. 79 (with separate English summary).

Jansen, M. *Der Fremdsprachenunterricht und die muttersprachliche Bildung.* (Empirische Untersuchungen). (Teaching of foreign language and mother tongue.) German summary of publication No. 79. Fremmedsprogs- og modersmålsundervisning. Copenhagen: Munksgaard, 1976.

Jansen, M. *Relations between the qualifications of different groups of readers and different aspects of given texts.* Congress paper read at the Processing of Visible Language Congress at Eindhoven, 1977. (mimeographed)

Jansen, M., J. Ahm, P. E. Jensen & A. Leerskov. Is special education necessary? – Can this program possibly be reduced? *Journal of learning disabilities,* 1970, *3*(9), 11–16.

Jansen, M. et al. New cities, educational traditions and the future. In: Lauwerys, J. A. & D. Scanlon (Eds.), *Education in cities.* London: The World Year Book of Education, 1970.

Jansen, M. & A. Leerskov. *Ti års tidsskriftartikler om danskundervisning børnehaveklasse – 7. skoleår. Registrering og analyse.* (Write-ups in periodicals over a ten-year period on the teaching of Danish. Registration and analysis.) Copenhagen: The Danish Institute for Educational Research, 1970. No. 71 (with English summary).

Jansen, M. & J. Ahm. *Arbejdsbøger til dansk, børnehaveklassen og 1.–7. skoleår. Registrering og analyse.* (Work books on the subject of Danish for the kindergarten class and the first seven grades – registration and analysis.) Copenhagen: The Danish Institute for Educational Research, 1971. No. 72 (with English summary).

Jansen, M. & Bjørn Glæsel. Hvordan læser og staver eleverne? – en sammenlignende status. (How do pupils read and spell? – a comparative statement). *Læsepædagogen,* 1977, 25 (4), 193–201.

Jansen, M. & S. Kreiner Møller. Who or what determines the activities of the classroom teacher? *Classroom Interaction Newsletter,* 1971, 7(1), 56–67.

Jansen, M., A. Søegård, M. Hansen & B. Glæsel. Special education in Denmark. In: Tarnopol, L. & M. *Reading disabilities.* Baltimore, Maryland: University Park Press, 1976. Offprint. 1973. The Danish Institute for Educational Research. No. 75

Jensen, P. E. *Klassestørrelser og undervisningsdifferentiering.* (Class size and individualization.) Copenhagen: Munksgaard, 1973. The Danish Institute of Educational Research. No. 75 (with English summary).

Larsen, A. Materiale til undervisning af ordblinde og læsesvage. (Material for instruction of the wordblind and retarded readers.) *Læsepædagogen,* 1952, *1*(1), 13–15

Larsen, C. A. *Om undervisning af børn med læse- og stavevanskeligheder i de første skoleår.* (On the instruction of children encountering difficulties in reading and spelling during the first few grades.) Copenhagen: The Danish Institute for Educational Research, 1960 (with English summary).

Lundahl, F. *Læsepædagogens materiale- og frilæsningsliste. (Læse-*

pædagogen's list of educational material and books for reading), 7th rev. ed. Dragør: Landsforeningen af Læsepædagoger, 1969.

Lundahl, F. *Materiale- og frilæsningsliste til undervisning i dansk 1.-7. skoleår og specialundervisning/175 lettere bøger til unge og voksne.* (List of materials and books for reading for the teaching of Danish in grades 1-7 and special reading training/ 175 easy books for young people and adults.) Copenhagen: Læsepædagogen, 1975.

Lundahl, F. *Liste over let faglig læsning og håndbøger i klassen.* (List of easy professional reading and manuals in the class.) Copenhagen: Læsepædagogen, 1976.

McDonald, A. S. & J. A. Byrne. Four questions on objectives. *Journal of Developmental Reading,* 1958, *1,* 46-51.

Maier, N. R. F. *Problem solving discussions and conferences.* New York: McGraw Hill, 1963.

Rasborg, F. *Undervisningsmetoder og arbejdsmønstre.* (Instructional methods and patterns of work.) Copenhagen: The Danish Institute for Educational Research, 1968. No. 67 (with English summary).

Raygor, A. L. Individualizing a college reading program. In Figurel, J. A. (Ed.), *Reading and inquiry.* International Reading Association Conference Proceedings, vol. 10. Newark, Del.: International Reading Association, 1965.

Robinson, F. P. *Effective study.* Rev. ed. New York: Harper & Row, 1961. p. 74

Rørdam, T. *The Danish folk high schools.* Copenhagen: Det Danske Selskab, 1965.

Shores, J. H. Dimensions of reading speed and comprehension. *Elementary English,* 1968, *45.*

Smith, D. E. P. Fit teaching methods to personality structure. *The High School Journal,* 1955, *40,* 167-171.

Spache, G. D. *Toward better reading.* Champaign, Ill.: Garrard Publishing Company, 1963.

Spache, G. D. Clinical work with college students. In: Leedy, P. D. (Ed.), *College-adult reading instruction.* Newark, Del.: International Reading Association, 1964. p. 321

Strang, R. The reading process and its ramifications. In: Dawson, M. A. (Ed.), *Developing comprehension including critical reading.* Newark, Del.: International Reading Association, 1968.

Stybe, V. Die Kinderbuchforschung in Dänemark auf dem historischen Gebiet. (Research into children's literature in the

174

historic perspective.) In *International symposium on children's literature*, Frankfurt 1971, 103–105.

Tarnopol, L. & M. *Reading disabilities.* Baltimore: University Park Press, 1976.

Thomsen, O. B. *Some aspects of education in Denmark.* Toronto: The Ontario Institute for Studies in Education, 1967.

Toffler, A. *Future shock.* London: Bodley Head, 1970.

Tordrup, S. A. Stavefejl og fejltyper hos elever fra 5. normalklasse og fra 5. og 6. læseklasse. (Spelling errors and types of errors made by pupils from the 5th normal grade and the 5th and 6th reading classes.) *Skolepsykologi,* 1965, *2*(1), 1–69 and 75–91.

Tordrup, S. A. Læseudviklingen hos elever med store læsevanskeligheder. (The development of reading among pupils experiencing great difficulties in reading.) *Skolepsykologi,* 1967, *4*(1), 1–154 (with English summary).

Undervisningsvejledning for folkeskolen II. (The national curriculum plan.) Betænkning nr. 297. Copenhagen: The Ministry of Education, 1961.

Vernon, M. D. *Visual perception and its relation to reading. An annotated bibliography.* Newark, Del.: International Reading Association, 1966, rev. 1969.

Zimet, Sara G. (Ed.) *What children read in school.* New York & London: Grune & Stratton, 1972

Zimet, S. G., G. E. Blom & R. R. Waite. *A teacher's guide for selecting stories for children. – The content of first grade reading textbooks.* Detroit: Wayne State University Press, 1968.

Zimet, S. G. Children's interests and story preferences; a critical review of the literature. *Elementary School Journal,* 1966, 67, 366–374

* The references listed here are of three types: 1) publications in Danish and other Scandinavian languages with titles also translated into English and some with an English summary, 2) publications in English and 3) publications in German with titles also translated into English.

Index

178

girls 46, 156
Glæsel, B. 46
government *144*
graphic pictures 41
Gray, W. S. 84
Greenland 28, 150
Greenlanders 28, 162
Grieg, N. 159
Grimm, J. & W. 157, 158
group conversation 166
   – discussion 117, 118
   – emotion 113
   – instruction 94, *116, 120,* 141, 142
   – interaction 118
guessing reading, see reading

H
habits 85, 124, 140, 166, 167
   –, reading, see reading
   –, study, see study
   –, work 98, 113, 118, *126,* 142
Hansen, E. J. 146
holistic approach 22, *23, 137*
   – psychology 20, *29,* 137
   – view 47, 140, 141, 142

I
Iceland 150
illustrations 31, 65, 156, 166
immediate appearance 47
immigrants 129
import 146
independent reading, see reading
individual 20, 27, 28, 33, 47, 57, 59, 61, 69, *95,* 118, 149
   – differences 120, 142
   – psychology 57
individualization 20, *22,* 27, 36, 37, *56, 57, 58, 62, 63, 65, 68,* 69,
   94, *120,* 137, *139*
industry 145
information units 80
inner voice 97, 105, 106, 109, 114, 115, 118, 122, 123, 125, 140, 166
inservice training 146
instructional discussions 99, *113,* 114, 115, *117, 118,* 141
intellectual development, see development

180

libraries *151*
  –, children's 65, 151
  –, school, see school
Lindgren, A. 157, 158
linguistic ability 32, 147
  – appearance 46, 48, 50
  – aspect 46
  – development, see development
  – factors *48*, 138
  – form 47
  – level 40
  – training, see training
listening *24*, 25, 137
list of materials, see material
literature 42, 77, 89, 97, 111, 133, 143, 150, 162
  –, professional 52
  –, self-chosen 39
long-term effect 165
lower secondary school, see school
Lundahl, F. 85, 154

M
magazines 39, 125, 150
Maier, N. R. F. 113
male 38, 149, 156
mass media 28
material *21*, 25, 29, 35, 43, 48, 54, *55*, 63, *65*, 85, 101, 139, 141, 152, 157, 164, 165, 169
  –, educational 31, 53, 62, 131, 133, 153, *155*
  –, learning 58
  –, reading, see reading
  –, study 33, 48
  –, teaching 34, *46*, 138
  –, training 37, 167
maturity 32, 42, 54
  – test, see test
McDonald, A. S. 68
mechanic *129*, 130, 143
mechanical learning apparatus 53
men 156, 160
method *21*, 29, 36, 40, 41, *54*, 58, *62*, 65, 68, *69*, 85, *87*, 90, *94*, 114, 127, 128, 135, 137, 138, 139, 140, *141*, 142, 143
  –, kinesthetic 54
  –, put in a slip of paper- 107, 111

182